Get Ready!

FOR STANDARDIZED TESTS

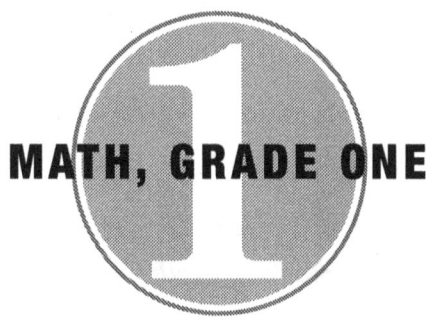

MATH, GRADE ONE

Other Books in the *Get Ready!* Series:

Get Ready! for Standardized Tests: Grade 1 by Joseph Harris, Ph.D.

Get Ready! for Standardized Tests: Grade 2 by Joseph Harris, Ph. D.

Get Ready! for Standardized Tests: Grade 3 by Karen Mersky, Ph.D.

Get Ready! for Standardized Tests: Grade 4 by Joseph Harris, Ph.D.

Get Ready! for Standardized Tests: Grade 5 by Leslie E. Talbott, Ph.D.

Get Ready! for Standardized Tests: Grade 6 by Shirley Vickery, Ph.D.

Get Ready! for Standardized Tests: Math, Grade 2 by Kristin Swanson

Get Ready! for Standardized Tests: Math, Grade 3 by Susan Osborne

Get Ready! for Standardized Tests: Math, Grade 4 by June Heller

Get Ready! for Standardized Tests: Reading, Grade 1 by Molly Maack

Get Ready! for Standardized Tests: Reading, Grade 2 by Louise Ulrich

Get Ready! for Standardized Tests: Reading, Grade 3 by Joanne Baker

Get Ready! for Standardized Tests: Reading, Grade 4 by Kris Callahan

TEST PREPARATION SERIES

Get Ready!

FOR STANDARDIZED TESTS

MATH, GRADE ONE

Sandy McConnell

Carol Turkington
Series Editor

McGraw-Hill

New York   Chicago   San Francisco
Lisbon   London   Madrid   Mexico City
Milan   New Delhi   San Juan   Seoul
Singapore   Sydney   Toronto

Library of Congress Cataloging-in-Publication Data

Get ready! for standardized tests. Math.
    p. cm.—(Test preparation series)
  Includes bibliographical references.
  Contents: [1] Grade 1 / Sandy McConnell—[2] Grade 2 / Kristin Swanson
  ISBN 0-07-137399-3 (pbk. : v. 1)—ISBN 0-07-137400-0 (pbk. : v. 2)
    1. Mathematics—Study and teaching (Elementary)—United States
  2. Mathematics—Study and teaching—Parent participation—United States   3. Achievement tests—United States—Study guides. I. McConnell, Sandy. II. Test preparation series (McGraw-Hill Companies)

QA135.6 .G47   2001
372.7—dc21   2001030901

McGraw-Hill

A Division of The McGraw·Hill Companies

Copyright © 2001 by The McGraw-Hill Companies, Inc. All rights reserved. Printed in the United States of America. Except as permitted under the United States Copyright Act of 1976, no part of this publication may be reproduced or distributed in any form or by any means, or stored in a data base or retrieval system, without the prior written permission of the publisher.

1 2 3 4 5 6 7 8 9 0 COU/COU 0 9 8 7 6 5 4 3 2 1

ISBN 0-07-137399-3

This book was set in New Century Schoolbook by Inkwell Publishing Services.

Printed and bound by Courier.

McGraw-Hill books are available at special quantity discounts to use as premiums and sales promotions, or for use in corporate training programs. For more information, please write to the Director of Special Sales, McGraw-Hill, Professional Publishing, Two Penn Plaza, New York, NY 10121-2298. Or contact your local bookstore.

Dedicated to the memory of Mary Jean Hart, my mother, my favorite teacher

Sandy McConnell

Contents

Skills Checklist   ix

Introduction   1
- Types of Standardized Tests   1
- The Major Standardized Tests   2
- How States Use Standardized Tests   2
- Valid Uses of Standardized Test Scores   3
- Inappropriate Use of Standardized Test Scores   3
- Two Basic Assumptions   4
- A Word about Coaching   4
- How to Raise Test Scores   4
- Test Questions   5

Chapter 1. Test-Taking Basics   7
- What This Book Can Do   7
- How to Use This Book   8
- Basic Test-Taking Strategies   8
- On to the Second Chapter   10

Chapter 2. Understanding Numbers and Patterns   11
- What First Graders Should Know   11
- What You and Your Child Can Do   12
- What Tests May Ask   14
- Practice Skill: Understanding Numbers and Patterns   14

Chapter 3. Addition   23
- What First Graders Should Know   23
  - Equal Sign   23
  - Sets   23
  - Zero Property of Addition   24
  - One Plus Rule   24
  - Communitive Property of Addition   24
  - Grouping Addition Facts   24
  - "Doubles" Addition Facts   24
  - "Doubles Plus One" Facts   25
  - The Nine Plus Rule   25
  - Counting On   25
  - Adding Three Numbers   25
  - Adding a Two-Digit Number to a Two-Digit Number   25
- What You and Your Child Can Do   26
- What Tests May Ask   27
- Practice Skill: Addition   27

Chapter 4. Subtraction   33
- What First Graders Should Know   33
  - Subtracting from a Two-Digit Number   33
- What You and Your Child Can Do   34
- What Tests May Ask   36
- Practice Skill: Subtraction   36

Chapter 5. Time: Clocks and Calendars   39
- Telling Time   39
  - What First Graders Should Know   39
  - What You and Your Child Can Do   40
  - What Tests May Ask   40
  - Practice Skill: Telling Time   40
- Calendars   42

What First Graders Should Know	42
What You and Your Child Can Do	42
What Tests May Ask	42
Practice Skill: Calendars	42

Chapter 6. Money — 45

What First Graders Should Know	45
Counting Money	45
What You and Your Child Can Do	46
What Tests May Ask	46
Practice Skill: Money	46

Chapter 7. Geometry — 51

What First Graders Should Know	51
What You and Your Child Can Do	51
Two-Dimensional Shapes	51
Three-Dimensional Shapes	52
Symmetry	53
Graphs	53
What Tests May Ask	54
Practice Skill: Geometry	54

Chapter 8. Fractions — 57

What First Graders Should Know	57
What You and Your Child Can Do	57
What Tests May Ask	58
Practice Skill: Fractions	58

Chapter 9. Measurement — 61

What First Graders Should Know	61
What You and Your Child Can Do	62
Measuring Length and Capacity	62
Measuring Mass (Weight)	63
What Tests May Ask	63
Practice Skill: Measuring	64

Chapter 10. Solving Word Problems — 69

What First Graders Should Know	69
What You and Your Child Can Do	70
What Tests May Ask	70
Practice Skill: Solving Word Problems	70

Appendix A: Web Sites and Resources for More Information — 75

Appendix B: Read More about It — 79

Appendix C: What Your Child's Test Scores Mean — 81

Appendix D: Which States Require Which Tests — 89

Appendix E: Testing Accommodations — 99

Glossary — 101

Answer Keys for Practice Skills — 103

Sample Practice Test — 105

Answer Key for Sample Practice Test — 127

MATH, GRADE ONE
SKILLS CHECKLIST

MY CHILD ...	HAS LEARNED	IS WORKING ON
NUMBERS AND PATTERNS		
ADDITION		
EQUAL SIGN		
SETS		
FACT FAMILIES		
PLACE VALUE		
SKIP COUNTING		
SUBTRACTION		
TELLING TIME		
CALENDARS		
NAMES AND VALUE OF COINS		
COUNTING MONEY		
CIRCLE		
SQUARE		
RECTANGLE		
TRIANGLE		
SYMMETRY		
FRACTIONS: $1/2$		
FRACTIONS: $1/3$ AND $2/3$		
FRACTIONS: $1/4$, $2/4$, $3/4$		
NONSTANDARD UNITS OF MEASUREMENT		
WEIGHING POUNDS		
WORD PROBLEMS		

Introduction

Almost all of us have taken standardized tests in school. We spent several days bubbling-in answers, shifting in our seats. No one ever told us why we took the tests or what they would do with the results. We just took them and never heard about them again.

Today many parents aren't aware they are entitled to see their children's permanent records and, at a reasonable cost, to obtain copies of any information not protected by copyright, including testing scores. Late in the school year, most parents receive standardized test results with confusing bar charts and detailed explanations of scores that few people seem to understand.

In response to a series of negative reports on the state of education in this country, Americans have begun to demand that something be done to improve our schools. We have come to expect higher levels of accountability as schools face the competing pressures of rising educational expectations and declining school budgets. High-stakes standardized tests are rapidly becoming the main tool of accountability for students, teachers, and school administrators. If students' test scores don't continually rise, teachers and principals face the potential loss of school funding and, ultimately, their jobs. Summer school and private after-school tutorial program enrollments are swelling with students who have not met score standards or who, everyone agrees, could score higher.

While there is a great deal of controversy about whether it is appropriate for schools to use standardized tests to make major decisions about individual students, it appears likely that standardized tests are here to stay. They will be used to evaluate students, teachers, and the schools; schools are sure to continue to use students' test scores to demonstrate their accountability to the community.

The purposes of this guide are to acquaint you with the types of standardized tests your children may take; to help you understand the test results; and to help you work with your children in skill areas that are measured by standardized tests so they can perform as well as possible.

Types of Standardized Tests

The two major types of group standardized tests are *criterion-referenced tests* and *norm-referenced tests*. Think back to when you learned to tie your shoes. First Mom or Dad showed you how to loosen the laces on your shoe so that you could insert your foot; then they showed you how to tighten the laces—but not too tight. They showed you how to make bows and how to tie a knot. All the steps we just described constitute what is called a *skills hierarchy:* a list of skills from easiest to most difficult that are related to some goal, such as tying a shoelace.

Criterion-referenced tests are designed to determine at what level students are performing on various skills hierarchies. These tests assume that development of skills follows a sequence of steps. For example, if you were teaching shoelace tying, the skills hierarchy might appear this way:

1. Loosen laces.
2. Insert foot.
3. Tighten laces.
4. Make loops with both lace ends.
5. Tie a square knot.

Criterion-referenced tests try to identify how far along the skills hierarchy the student has progressed. There is no comparison against anyone else's score, only against an expected skill level. The main question criterion-referenced tests ask is: "Where is this child in the development of this group of skills?"

Norm-referenced tests, in contrast, are typically constructed to compare children in their abilities as to different skills areas. Although the experts who design test items may be aware of skills hierarchies, they are more concerned with how much of some skill the child has mastered, rather than at what level on the skills hierarchy the child is.

Ideally, the questions on these tests range from very easy items to those that are impossibly difficult. The essential feature of norm-referenced tests is that scores on these measures can be compared to scores of children in similar groups. They answer this question: "How does the child compare with other children of the same age or grade placement in the development of this skill?"

This book provides strategies for increasing your child's scores on both standardized norm-referenced and criterion-referenced tests.

The Major Standardized Tests

Many criterion-referenced tests currently in use are created locally or (at best) on a state level, and there are far too many of them to go into detail here about specific tests. However, children prepare for them in basically the same way they do for norm-referenced tests.

A very small pool of norm-referenced tests is used throughout the country, consisting primarily of the Big Five:

- California Achievement Tests (CTB/McGraw-Hill)
- Iowa Tests of Basic Skills (Riverside)
- Metropolitan Achievement Test (Harcourt-Brace & Company)
- Stanford Achievement Test (Psychological Corporation)
- TerraNova [formerly Comprehensive Test of Basic Skills] (McGraw-Hill)

These tests use various terms for the academic skills areas they assess, but they generally test several types of reading, language, and mathematics skills, along with social studies and science. They may include additional assessments, such as of study and reference skills.

How States Use Standardized Tests

Despite widespread belief and practice to the contrary, group standardized tests are designed to assess and compare the achievement of groups. They are *not* designed to provide detailed diagnostic assessments of individual students. (For detailed individual assessments, children should be given individual diagnostic tests by properly qualified professionals, including trained guidance counselors, speech and language therapists, and school psychologists.) Here are examples of the types of questions group standardized tests are designed to answer:

- How did the reading achievement of students at Valley Elementary School this year compare with their reading achievement last year?

INTRODUCTION

- How did math scores at Wonderland Middle School compare with those of students at Parkside Middle School this year?
- As a group, how did Hilltop High School students compare with the national averages in the achievement areas tested?
- How did the district's first graders' math scores compare with the district's fifth graders' math scores?

The fact that these tests are designed primarily to test and compare groups doesn't mean that test data on individual students isn't useful. It does mean that when we use these tests to diagnose individual students, we are using them for a purpose for which they were not designed.

Think of group standardized tests as being similar to health fairs at the local mall. Rather than check into your local hospital and spend thousands of dollars on full, individual tests for a wide range of conditions, you can go from station to station and take part in different health screenings. Of course, one would never diagnose heart disease or cancer on the basis of the screening done at the mall. At most, suspicious results on the screening would suggest that you need to visit a doctor for a more complete examination.

In the same way, group standardized tests provide a way of screening the achievement of many students quickly. Although you shouldn't diagnose learning problems solely based on the results of these tests, the results can tell you that you should think about referring a child for a more definitive, individual assessment.

An individual student's group test data should be considered only a point of information. Teachers and school administrators may use standardized test results to support or question hypotheses they have made about students; but these scores must be used alongside other information, such as teacher comments, daily work, homework, class test grades, parent observations, medical needs, and social history.

Valid Uses of Standardized Test Scores

Here are examples of appropriate uses of test scores for individual students:

- Mr. Cone thinks that Samantha, a third grader, is struggling in math. He reviews her file and finds that her first- and second-grade standardized test math scores were very low. Her first- and second-grade teachers recall episodes in which Samantha cried because she couldn't understand certain math concepts, and mention that she was teased by other children, who called her "Dummy." Mr. Cone decides to refer Samantha to the school assistance team to determine whether she should be referred for individual testing for a learning disability related to math.

- The local college wants to set up a tutoring program for elementary school children who are struggling academically. In deciding which youngsters to nominate for the program, the teachers consider the students' averages in different subjects, the degree to which students seem to be struggling, parents' reports, and standardized test scores.

- For the second year in a row, Gene has performed poorly on the latest round of standardized tests. His teachers all agree that Gene seems to have some serious learning problems. They had hoped that Gene was immature for his class and that he would do better this year; but his dismal grades continue. Gene is referred to the school assistance team to determine whether he should be sent to the school psychologist for assessment of a possible learning handicap.

Inappropriate Use of Standardized Test Scores

Here are examples of how schools have sometimes used standardized test results inappropriately:

- Mr. Johnson groups his students into reading groups solely on the basis of their standardized test scores.
- Ms. Henry recommends that Susie be held back a year because she performed poorly on the standardized tests, despite strong grades on daily assignments, homework, and class tests.
- Gerald's teacher refers him for consideration in the district's gifted program, which accepts students using a combination of intelligence test scores, achievement test scores, and teacher recommendations. Gerald's intelligence test scores were very high. Unfortunately, he had a bad cold during the week of the standardized group achievement tests and was taking powerful antihistamines, which made him feel sleepy. As a result, he scored too low on the achievement tests to qualify.

The public has come to demand increasingly high levels of accountability for public schools. We demand that schools test so that we have hard data with which to hold the schools accountable. But too often, politicians and the public place more faith in the test results than is justified. Regardless of whether it's appropriate to do so and regardless of the reasons schools use standardized test results as they do, many schools base crucial programming and eligibility decisions on scores from group standardized tests. It's to your child's advantage, then, to perform as well as possible on these tests.

Two Basic Assumptions

The strategies we present in this book come from two basic assumptions:

1. Most students can raise their standardized test scores.
2. Parents can help their children become stronger in the skills the tests assess.

This book provides the information you need to learn what skill areas the tests measure, what general skills your child is being taught in a particular grade, how to prepare your child to take the tests, and what to do with the results. In the appendices you will find information to help you decipher test interpretations; a listing of which states currently require what tests; and additional resources to help you help your child to do better in school and to prepare for the tests.

A Word about Coaching

This guide is *not* about coaching your child. When we use the term *coaching* in referring to standardized testing, we mean trying to give someone an unfair advantage, either by revealing beforehand what exact items will be on the test or by teaching "tricks" that will supposedly allow a student to take advantage of some detail in how the tests are constructed.

Some people try to coach students in shrewd test-taking strategies that take advantage of how the tests are supposedly constructed rather than strengthening the students' skills in the areas tested. Over the years, for example, many rumors have been floated about "secret formulas" that test companies use.

This type of coaching emphasizes ways to help students obtain scores they didn't earn—to get something for nothing. Stories have appeared in the press about teachers who have coached their students on specific questions, parents who have tried to obtain advance copies of tests, and students who have written down test questions after taking standardized tests and sold them to others. Because of the importance of test security, test companies and states aggressively prosecute those who attempt to violate test security—and they should do so.

How to Raise Test Scores

Factors that are unrelated to how strong students are but that might artificially lower test scores include anything that prevents students from making scores that accurately describe their actual abilities. Some of those factors are:

- giving the tests in uncomfortably cold or hot rooms;
- allowing outside noises to interfere with test taking; and
- reproducing test booklets in such small print or with such faint ink that students can't read the questions.

Such problems require administrative attention from both the test publishers, who must make sure that they obtain their norms for the tests under the same conditions students face when they take the tests; and school administrators, who must ensure that conditions under which their students take the tests are as close as possible to those specified by the test publishers.

Individual students also face problems that can artificially lower their test scores, and parents can do something about many of these problems. Stomach aches, headaches, sleep deprivation, colds and flu, and emotional upsets due to a recent tragedy are problems that might call for the student to take the tests during make-up sessions. Some students have physical conditions such as muscle-control problems, palsies, or difficulty paying attention that require work over many months or even years before students can obtain accurate test scores on standardized tests. And, of course, some students just don't take the testing seriously or may even intentionally perform poorly. Parents can help their children overcome many of these obstacles to obtaining accurate scores.

Finally, with this book parents are able to help their children raise their scores by:

- increasing their familiarity (and their comfort level) with the types of questions on standardized tests;
- drills and practice exercises to increase their skill in handling the kinds of questions they will meet; and
- providing lots of fun ways for parents to help their children work on the skill areas that will be tested.

Test Questions

The favorite type of question for standardized tests is the multiple-choice question. For example:

1. The first President of the United States was:

   A Abraham Lincoln

   B Martin Luther King, Jr.

   C George Washington

   D Thomas Jefferson

The main advantage of multiple-choice questions is that it is easy to score them quickly and accurately. They lend themselves to optical scanning test forms, on which students fill in bubbles or squares and the forms are scored by machine. Increasingly, companies are moving from paper-based testing to computer-based testing, using multiple-choice questions.

The main disadvantage of multiple-choice questions is that they restrict test items to those that can be put in that form. Many educators and civil rights advocates have noted that the multiple-choice format only reveals a superficial understanding of the subject. It's not possible with multiple-choice questions to test a student's ability to construct a detailed, logical argument on some issue or to explain a detailed process. Although some of the major tests are beginning to incorporate more subjectively scored items, such as short answer or essay questions, the vast majority of test items continue to be in multiple-choice format.

In the past, some people believed there were special formulas or tricks to help test-takers determine which multiple-choice answer was the correct one. There may have been some truth to *some* claims for past tests. Computer analyses of some past tests revealed certain biases in how tests were constructed. For example, the old advice to pick *D* when in doubt appears to have been valid for some past tests. However, test publishers have become so sophisticated in their ability to detect patterns of bias in the formulation of test questions and answers that they now guard against it aggressively.

In Chapter 1, we provide information about general test-taking considerations, with advice on how parents can help students overcome testing obstacles. The rest of the book provides information to help parents help their children strengthen skills in the tested areas.

Joseph Harris, Ph.D.

Test-Taking Basics

At some point during the 12 years that your children spend in school, they'll face a standardized testing situation. Some schools test every year, some test every other year—but eventually your child will be assessed. How well your child does on such a test can be related to many things—Did he get plenty of rest the night before? Is she anxious in testing situations? Did he get confused when filling in the answer sheets and make a mechanical mistake? That's why educators emphasize that a child's score on a standardized test shouldn't be used as the sole judge of how that child is learning and developing. Instead, the scores should be evaluated as only one part of the educational picture, together with the child's classroom performance and overall areas of strength and weakness. Your child won't pass or fail a standardized test, but often you can see a general pattern of strengths and weaknesses.

Although most states don't require standardized testing in first grade, it is important for children to become familiar with the testing situation as early as possible in order to build confidence for required testing in later grades.

Keep in mind, however, that the format for standardized tests may differ slightly from one test to another. While this book offers your child exposure to typical sample questions that may appear on the tests, it's difficult to provide samples common to all. Keep this in mind, and don't make your children practice *too* much—or they may become alarmed when the "real test" is not exactly like the questions they have seen in this book. "Guiding" is the key here—if your child understands the basic concepts, she will be successful regardless of the format.

What This Book Can Do

This book is not designed to help your child artificially inflate scores on a standardized test. Instead, it's intended to help you understand the typical kinds of skills taught in a first-grade class and what a typical first grader can be expected to know by the end of the first year. It also presents lots of fun activities that you can use at home to work with your child in particular skill areas that may be a bit weak.

Of course, this book should not be used to replace your child's teacher. It should be used as a guide to help you work together with the school as a team to help your child succeed. Keep in mind, however, that endless drilling is not the best way to help your child improve. While most children want to do well and please their teachers and parents, they already spend about 7 hours a day in school. Extracurricular activities, homework, music, and play take up more time. Try to use the activities in this book to stimulate and support your children's work at school, not to overwhelm them.

Most children entering the first grade are eager to learn. One of the most serious mistakes that many parents of children this age make is to try to get their children to master skills for which they aren't developmentally ready. For example, while most children this age are ready to read, some aren't, and no amount of drill will make them ready to read.

There's certainly nothing wrong with working with your child, but if you're trying to teach the same skill over and over and your child just isn't "getting it," you may be trying to teach something that your child just isn't ready for.

You may notice that your child still seems a bit clumsy and still has problems coloring within the lines. Symbolic reasoning begins to appear in first grade, as children start to learn that printed numbers stand for numerals—that 5 means five. As the year progresses, your first grader will become more and more able to recognize abstract qualities and to consider more than one characteristic at one time.

Remember, however, that not all children learn things at the same rate. What may be typical for one first grader is certainly not typical for another. You should use the information presented in this book in conjunction with school work to help develop your child's essential skills in mathematics and number skills.

How to Use This Book

There are many different ways to use this book. Some children are quite strong in certain math areas but need a bit of help in other areas. Perhaps your child is a whiz at adding but has more trouble with telling time. Focus your attention on those skills which need some work, and spend more time on those areas. You'll see in each chapter an introductory explanation of the material in the chapter, followed by a summary of what a typical child in first grade should be expected to know about that skill by the end of the year. This is followed in each chapter by an extensive section featuring interesting, fun, or unusual activities you can do with your child to reinforce the skills presented in the chapter. Most use only inexpensive items found around the home, and many are suitable for car trips, waiting rooms, and restaurants.

Next, you'll find an explanation of how typical standardized tests may assess that skill and what your child might expect to see on a typical test.

We've included sample questions at the end of each section that are designed to help familiarize your child with the types of questions found on a typical standardized test. These questions do *not* measure your child's proficiency in any given content area—but if you notice that your child is having trouble with a particular question, you can use the information to figure out what skills you need to focus on.

Basic Test-Taking Strategies

Sometimes children score lower on standardized tests because they approach testing in an inefficient way. There are things you can do before the test—and that your child can do during the test—to make sure that he does as well as he can. There are a few things you might want to remember about standardized tests. One is that they can only ask a limited number of questions dealing with each skill before they run out of paper. On most tests, the total math component is made up of about 60 items and takes about 90 minutes. In some cases, your child may encounter only one exercise evaluating a particular skill. An important practice area that is often overlooked is the *listening* element of the tests. Most of the math questions are done as a group and are read to the students by the proctor of the test, who is almost always the classroom teacher.

You can practice listening skills by reading the directions to each question to your child. Sometimes the instructions are so brief and to the point that they are almost too simple. In some cases, teachers are not permitted to reword or explain; they may read only what is written in the test manual. Usually, questions and directions or instructions may be repeated only one time. Read the directions as they have been given on the practice pages and then have your child explain to you what they mean. Then you'll both be clear about what the tests actually require.

TEST-TAKING BASICS

Before the Test

Perhaps the most effective thing you can do to prepare your child for standardized tests is to be patient and positive. Remember that no matter how much pressure you put on your children, they won't learn certain skills until they are physically, mentally, and emotionally ready to do so. You've got to walk a delicate line between challenging and pressuring your children. If children view testing as a "big, bad wolf," then they may develop negative attitudes that could affect their performance. If you see that your child isn't making progress or is getting frustrated, it may be time to lighten up.

Don't Change the Routine. Many experts offer mistaken advice about how to prepare children for a test, such as recommending that children go to bed early the night before or eat a high-protein breakfast on the morning of the test. It's a better idea not to alter your child's routine at all right before the test.

If your child isn't used to going to bed early, then sending him off at 7:30 p.m. the night before a test will only make it harder for him to get to sleep by the normal time. If he is used to eating an orange or a piece of toast for breakfast, forcing him to down a platter of fried eggs and bacon will only make him feel sleepy or uncomfortable.

Neatness. There is an incorrect way to fill in an answer sheet on a standardized test, and if this happens to your child, it can really make a difference on the final results. It pays to give your child some practice on filling in answer sheets. Watch how neatly your child can fill in the bubbles, squares, and rectangles below. If he overlaps the lines, makes a lot of erase marks, or presses the pencil too hard, try having him practice with pages of bubbles. You can easily create sheets of capital O's, squares, and rectangles that your child can practice filling in. If he gets bored doing that, have him color in detailed pictures in coloring books or complete connect-the-dots pages.

During the Test

There are some approaches to standardized testing that have been shown to make some degree of improvement in a score. Discuss the following strategies with your child from time to time.

Bring Extra Pencils. You don't want your child spending valuable testing time jumping up to sharpen a pencil. Send along plenty of extra, well-sharpened pencils, and your child will have more time to work on test questions.

Listen Carefully. You wouldn't believe how many errors kids make by not listening to instructions or not paying attention to demonstrations. Some children mark the wrong form, fill in the bubbles incorrectly, or skip to the wrong section. Others simply forget to include their names. Many make a mark without realizing whether they are marking the right bubble.

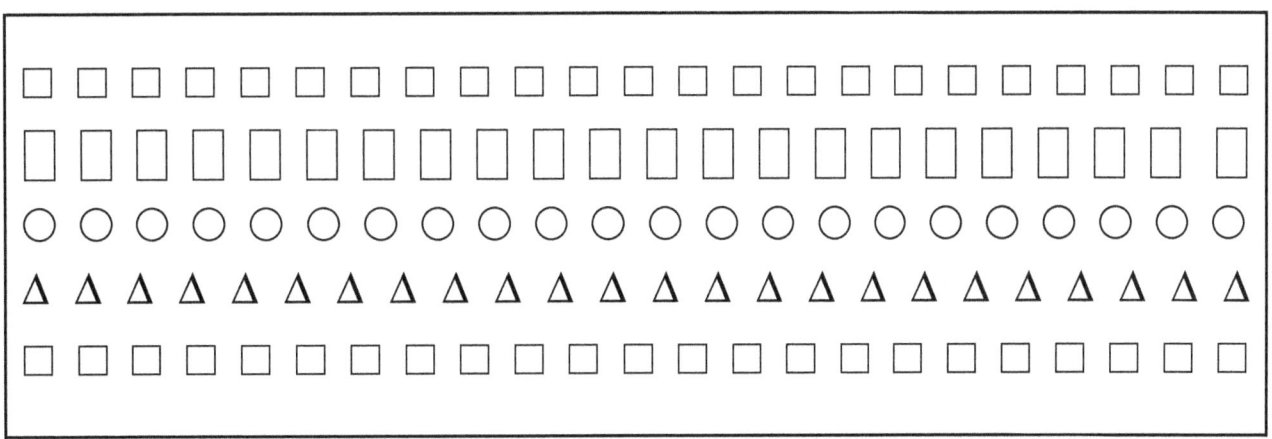

Read the Entire Question First. Some children get so excited about the test that they begin filling in the bubble before they finish reading the entire question. The last few words in a question sometimes give the most important clues to the correct answer.

Read Carefully. In their desire to finish first, many children tend to select the first answer that seems right to them without thoroughly reading all the responses and choosing the very best answer. Make sure your child understands the importance of evaluating all the answers before choosing one.

Write It Down. Most standardized tests allow children to use scratch paper for the math portion or to work directly in their test booklet. Encourage your child to write it down and work it out whenever appropriate. This would include computation for word problems given horizontally

$$53 + 24 = \underline{}$$

that can be solved easier if rewritten vertically

$$\begin{array}{r} 53 \\ +\ 24 \\ \hline \end{array}$$

Skip Difficult Items; Return Later. Many children will sit and worry about a hard question, spending so much time on one problem that they never get to problems that they would be able to answer correctly if they only had left enough time. Explain to your child that he can always come back to a knotty question once he finishes the section.

Refer to Pictures for Clues. Tell your child not to overlook the pictures in the test booklets, which may reveal valuable clues that he can use to help him find the correct answers. Students also can find clues to correct answers by looking at descriptions, wording, and other information in the questions.

Use Key Words. Have your child look at the questions and try to figure out the parts that are important and those that aren't.

Eliminate Answer Choices. Just like in the wildly successful TV show *Who Wants to Be a Millionaire,* remind your child that it's a good idea to narrow down his choices among multiple-choice options by eliminating answers he knows can't possibly be true. Emphasize that there should be only one answer marked for each question.

On to the Second Chapter

Now that you've learned a bit about the test-taking basics, it's time to turn your attention to the first of the math skills—understanding numbers and patterns.

CHAPTER 2

Understanding Numbers and Patterns

Whether it's age, number of brothers or sisters, or how many days until a holiday, your child has been exposed to numbers at a very early age. A child sees numerals on televisions, mailboxes, clocks, and phones. When numerals are associated with real-life experiences or concrete objects, a child sees the relevance—and understanding begins to develop. You want to be sure that this continues, so surround your child with numbers and involve her in their everyday functions.

Mathematics is the science of patterns, and you can train your child to be a "pattern detector." Through guided experiences, your child can discover the patterns in the world around her (especially the base 10 number system). This will build a good foundation and allow her to understand future math concepts. The ability to continue a pattern requires a child to analyze and sort information and make generalizations. Based on these generalizations, she makes predictions about how to continue a pattern. For example, when presented with the numbers 2, 2, 3, 2, 2, 3, your child should look at all the numbers given and try to discover what pattern is formed in order to arrive at the number that should appear next. After sorting the information, she should see that the pattern 2, 2, 3 is repeated and be able to make the generalization that 2, 2, 3 is going to be repeated over and over and that the numbers should continue to appear in that order. A child can learn the skills involved in patterning by using objects in her environment. Patterns can be found all around us in areas other than math, such as nature, art, music, and reading. Learning to see and understand patterns helps children to see relationships between information in our world, and this, in turn, produces logical thinkers. Children who look for patterns are usually more persistent and are less prone to frustration as math students.

What First Graders Should Know

First-grade children are expected to rote count (count by memory) from 1 to 100 and to be able to recognize and write the numerals from 1 to 100. Don't worry if your child reverses the numerals 2, 5, 7, or 9. With increased practice, these reversals usually occur less frequently and eventually are eliminated.

Children are expected to be able to count sets of up to 20 objects and write the numeral representing the number of objects in the set. They should be able to skip count by twos, fives, and tens to 100 (2, 4, 6; 5, 10, 15; or 10, 20, 30; and so on). Understanding the patterns in our base 10 number system and seeing the relationships between the numbers will enable them to be able to perform skip counting and also enable them to complete a sequence of skip counting backwards, such as 25, 20, 15, ... Given a set of numbers or objects, children should be able to extend a pattern.

Children also should be familiar with ordinal numbers from first to twentieth. (An *ordinal number* is the number listing the order in which an object appears in a series, such as "first," "second," and so on.) For example, when shown a picture of eight dogs in a line, your child should be able to identify the "third" dog.

Comprehending place value of the ones, tens, and hundreds is also a concept that should be grasped in mid-first grade. When a child sees the numeral "27," she should be able to understand that the "2" represents two tens and the "7" represents seven ones. Finally, your child should understand the concepts of "greater than" and "less than" and be able to state those relationships between any two numbers from 1 to 100.

What You and Your Child Can Do

Rote Counting. Expose your child to as many counting experiences as possible through the use of finger plays, counting songs, and nursery rhymes. These provide excitement and fun while learning to count forward and backward. "Ten Little Indians," "This Old Man," "One, Two, Buckle My Shoe," "Five Little Ducks," and "Roll Over, Roll Over" all help a child learn how to rote count.

Counting Objects. To learn how to count objects, your child first needs to know how to rote count. In addition to rote counting, she must incorporate the concept of one-to-one correspondence. This means that every time she says a number, she should point to only one object. The number of objects in the set is the last number she states. Encourage your child to count her toy cars, crayons, snacks, or books. Completing a household chore such as setting the table helps to enhance her understanding of one-to-one correspondence.

Counting Books. Help your child check out counting books such as *Ten Black Dots* by Donald Crews or *Fish Eyes* by Lois Ehlert in the library, and read them together.

Games. Many beginner board games, such as "Chutes and Ladders" or "Uncle Wiggly," will provide excellent practice counting and help your child become familiar with numbers.

Create a Book. Cut out pictures from a magazine, and create your own counting book. The first page should contain the numeral 1 and a picture of one object. The second page should contain the numeral 2 and a picture of two objects. Continue the pattern.

Play and Write. Write numerals in pudding, powdered Jell-O, sand, colored glue, paint, chalk, or glue and glitter.

Dough Numerals. Create numerals using Play-Doh or bread dough, and bake your number! Help your child pour out pancake batter into numbers and eat her handiwork.

Base 10 Patterns. The "Hundred Board," a 10 × 10 grid of numbers from 1 to 100, is a valuable tool to help your child understand the number system. You can buy one or make your own—you can easily draw a 10 × 10 grid. The first line should contain the numbers from 1 to 10; the second line should include 11 through 20, and so on to 100. It is well worth the effort to construct one; it will allow your child to discover for herself the patterns inherent in the number system. Complete the activities below using your "Hundred Board," and use M&M's, Cheerios, Smarties, or corn kernels to serve as markers. Have fun!

1. Mark the numbers 6, 16, 26, 36, 46, and 56. Do you see a pattern? What do all the numbers end with? What pattern do you see on the number board? (All the numbers that end the same are in the same column.)

2. Mark the numbers 21, 22, 23, 24, 25, 26, and 27. Do you see a pattern? What do all the numbers begin with? Do you see a pattern? Is there a number in the row that does not fit the pattern?

UNDERSTANDING NUMBERS AND PATTERNS

3. Mark the number 8. What number is one less than 8? Mark the number 42. What number is one less than 42? Mark the number 85. What number is one less than 85? Do you see a pattern?

4. Mark the number 36. What number is one more than 36? Mark the number 9. What number is one more than 9? Mark the number 93. What number is one more than 93? Do you see a pattern?

5. Play "Guess My Number." Using the "Hundred Board," ask the following questions: I'm thinking of a number that is one less than 12. What is my number? I'm thinking of a number that is between 15 and 17. What is my number? I'm thinking of a number that is two more than 76. What is my number?

6. Take a piece of paper and cover all the numbers except the numbers that end with 0. Read all the uncovered numbers. You are counting by tens!

7. Find the number 20. What is 10 more than 20? Find the number 15. What is 10 more than 15? Find the number 78. What is 10 more than 78? Your child may need to count 10 places after the given number in order to find the answer, but after several repetitions, she should discover that by adding 10 to a number, she just needs to find the number on the "Hundred Board" that is directly below the original number. This is the pattern. This generalization will come in very handy when your child learns to add tens to a number that ends with a five.

8. Cut two pieces of paper to a length and width that only covers the first four columns (the numbers that end with 1, 2, 3, and 4) and the sixth column through the ninth column (the numbers that end with 6, 7, 8, and 9). Practice reading them. Your child is counting by fives!

9. Cut strips of paper and cover the first, third, fifth, seventh, and ninth columns. Read the numbers. Practice counting by twos. Another way to practice skip counting is through the use of a calculator. To count by fives, have your child "tap in" 0 + 5 = = = = = =. Allow her to guess the number first and then tap the equal sign. If she can't guess, have her read the numbers as they appear each time the equal sign is tapped. This repetition will help her learn how to skip count by fives. To count by twos, tap in 0 + 2 (your constant) = = = = . Each time the equal sign is tapped, two will be added to the preceding number. Try to skip count by tens.

100 Hungry Ants. Read this book by Elinor Pinczes, and have your child arrange raisins or minimarshmallows in the same formations made by the ants in the book. She can explore the number 100 by arranging 100 items in different groups. She will group them into equal lines: one line, two lines, four lines, five lines, and finally, ten lines.

Hundreds of Things. Find objects such as cotton balls, stickers, stars, pennies, or toothpicks and arrange them on poster board in 10 groups of tens. Count by tens to 100. Your child will be able to visualize what 100 items looks like.

Learning to Write to 100. Help your child discover the pattern that when she counts to 100, the numbers 0 to 9 are repeated over and over, first by themselves and then preceded by a one, then a two, then a three, and so on. She should begin writing the numerals on a 10 × 10 grid in order for her to be able to correct her work by checking that all the numbers in the first column end with a zero and that each number in a row (except the first row) begins with the same numeral.

Place Value. Emphasize to your child that the magic number in the number system is 10. You can buy base 10 blocks or make your own manipulatives. Explain that counting is made easier by grouping things into tens. Take a handful of about 35 straws (or any similar object that can be bundled), and ask your child to count by ones to find out how many objects you gave her. Now have her group the straws in "bundles" of 10 by banding them together. If she doesn't have enough to make a group of 10, those are considered "ones."

Now ask her to count the objects. Count the bundles by 10, and add on the ones left over to arrive at the correct number, counting 30, 31, 32, 33, 34, 35.

Have her write the number, pointing out the tens column and the ones column. The 3 represents three bundles or three tens, and the 5 represents five singles or five ones. Writing the number helps her link her experience with the straws to the written number.

Discover how grouping objects makes counting much easier. Make ten bundles and leave nine unbundled or in ones. Count the bundles by counting by tens. Ask your child to find 62. She should select six bundles and two ones. Practice writing each number after she makes that number with the straws. Have her find 50, 28, 18, and 37 and practice until she feels comfortable with this concept.

Show her the numeral 52, and have her select the straws she needs to make a match. She should select five bundles and two singles. Connect this learning with the "Hundred Board," and play "Guess My Number": I'm thinking of a number that is 2 tens and 4 ones. Mark my number. I'm thinking of a number that is 5 tens and 0 ones. Mark my number.

Patterns Using Objects. Children can learn the skills involved in patterning by using objects in their environment. Use objects that differ by one attribute such as color, shape, or size, such as M&M's, Legos, or any item that differs by color only, or buy pattern blocks. Begin a pattern, and have your child continue it: red, brown, brown, red, brown, brown, ____. Remind her to use every part of information she was given. Point to every item from the beginning of the pattern, and state the important attribute that makes it different, and then continue the pattern. The attribute of shape can be used by cutting three different shapes out of paper and making a pattern: circle, triangle, square, circle, triangle, square, circle, ____.

What Tests May Ask

A standardized test may ask any number of questions dealing with basic facts, but time and space on the test limit the number of items pertaining to one particular concept. Your child should be prepared to

- count objects and choose the matching numeral.
- compare sets of objects.
- list numbers in order.
- skip count by twos, fives, and tens.

Practice Skill: Understanding Numbers and Patterns

Directions: Look at the picture and listen carefully to the question. Darken in the bubble beside your answer.

UNDERSTANDING NUMBERS AND PATTERNS

Example:

How many cars are there here?

- Ⓐ 3
- Ⓑ 5
- Ⓒ 7
- Ⓓ 6

Answer:

- Ⓑ 5

1. How many dogs are there here?
   - Ⓐ 7
   - Ⓑ 9
   - Ⓒ 8
   - Ⓓ 10

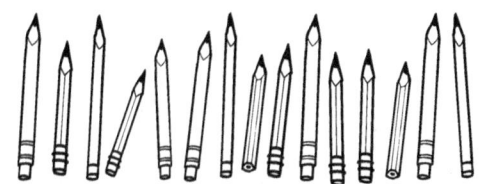

2. How many pencils are there here?
   - Ⓐ 15
   - Ⓑ 12
   - Ⓒ 16
   - Ⓓ 13

3. Which picture has the same number of balls as there are bats?

   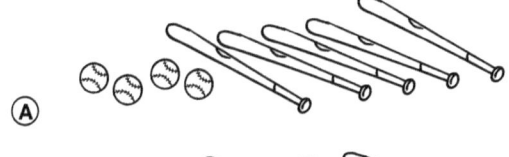
   Ⓐ

   Ⓑ

   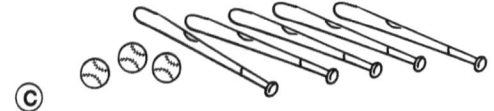
   Ⓒ

   Ⓓ

4 Which set of cars is two less than the number of houses?

Ⓐ

Ⓑ

Ⓒ

Ⓓ

5 How many more stars are needed to make the sets equal?

Ⓐ 1
Ⓑ 2
Ⓒ 3
Ⓓ 4

6 How many more balls are needed to make the sets equal?

Ⓐ 1
Ⓑ 2
Ⓒ 3
Ⓓ 4

7 Fill in the missing number: 36, 37, 38, 39, __, 41.

Ⓐ 30
Ⓑ 40
Ⓒ 42
Ⓓ 93

UNDERSTANDING NUMBERS AND PATTERNS

8 Fill in the missing number: 66, 67, __, 69.
- Ⓐ 65
- Ⓑ 70
- Ⓒ 76
- Ⓓ 68

9 What number is between 28 and 30?
- Ⓐ 31
- Ⓑ 27
- Ⓒ 40
- Ⓓ 29

10 What number is closest to 84?
- Ⓐ 48
- Ⓑ 90
- Ⓒ 82
- Ⓓ 87

11 What number is more than 46 and less than 51?
- Ⓐ 45
- Ⓑ 52
- Ⓒ 48
- Ⓓ 64

12 What number comes just before 80?
- Ⓐ 79
- Ⓑ 81
- Ⓒ 70
- Ⓓ 69

13 What number comes right after 12 when counting by ones?
- Ⓐ 21
- Ⓑ 13
- Ⓒ 11
- Ⓓ 18

14 What number is between 16 and 20?
- Ⓐ 18
- Ⓑ 61
- Ⓒ 21
- Ⓓ 14

15 Count by tens. Which number is missing? 20, __, 40, 50, 60
- Ⓐ 70
- Ⓑ 30
- Ⓒ 25
- Ⓓ 10

16 Count by twos. What number is missing? 2, 4, 6, __, 10
- Ⓐ 8
- Ⓑ 7
- Ⓒ 9
- Ⓓ 12

17 Count by fives. What number is missing? 5, 10, __, 20, 25
- Ⓐ 30
- Ⓑ 15
- Ⓒ 13
- Ⓓ 52

18 Count by tens backward. What comes after 60?
- Ⓐ 70
- Ⓑ 10
- Ⓒ 50
- Ⓓ 55

19 Count by twos backward. What number comes next? 8, 6, 4, __
- Ⓐ 6
- Ⓑ 3
- Ⓒ 10
- Ⓓ 2

20 Continue the pattern. 4, 2, 2, 4, 2, 2, 4, __, __.
- Ⓐ 2, 2
- Ⓑ 4, 4
- Ⓒ 2, 4
- Ⓓ 4, 2

21 Look at the picture above. Continue the pattern.
- Ⓐ
- Ⓑ
- Ⓒ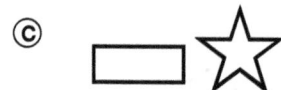
- Ⓓ

UNDERSTANDING NUMBERS AND PATTERNS

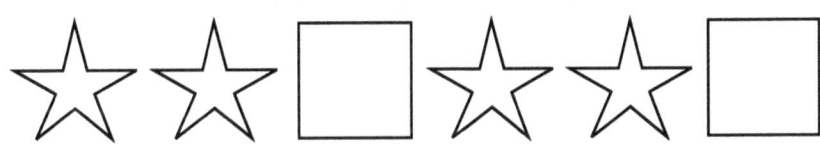

22 Look at the picture above. Continue the pattern.

23 What number has a 6 in the tens place?
- Ⓐ 63
- Ⓑ 26
- Ⓒ 33
- Ⓓ 635

24 How many tens are in 83?
- Ⓐ 11 tens
- Ⓑ 8 tens
- Ⓒ 3 tens
- Ⓓ 5 tens

25 Which number is equal to 4 tens?
- Ⓐ 4
- Ⓑ 400
- Ⓒ 40
- Ⓓ 44

26 How many ones are in the number 32?
- Ⓐ 5 ones
- Ⓑ 1 ones
- Ⓒ 3 ones
- Ⓓ 2 ones

27 What number has 1 ten and 2 ones?
- Ⓐ 3
- Ⓑ 12
- Ⓒ 21
- Ⓓ 11

28 What number has 5 tens and 9 ones?
- Ⓐ 50
- Ⓑ 59
- Ⓒ 95
- Ⓓ 14

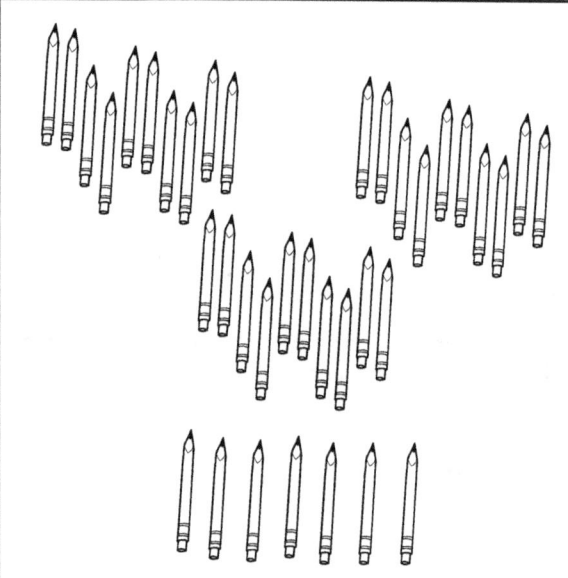

29 Look at the picture above. How many are there in all?
- Ⓐ 10
- Ⓑ 27
- Ⓒ 37
- Ⓓ 73

30 Which is the greatest number?
- Ⓐ 24
- Ⓑ 42
- Ⓒ 8
- Ⓓ 40

31 Which is the smallest number?
- Ⓐ 64
- Ⓑ 46
- Ⓒ 40
- Ⓓ 60

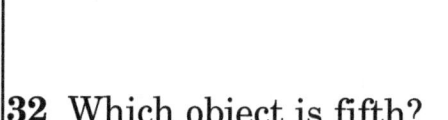

32 Which object is fifth?
- Ⓐ
- Ⓑ
- Ⓒ
- Ⓓ

UNDERSTANDING NUMBERS AND PATTERNS

33 To which ball does the arrow point?
- Ⓐ sixth
- Ⓑ second
- Ⓒ third
- Ⓓ fourth

(See page 103 for answer key.)

CHAPTER 3

Addition

Addition builds on the skill of counting objects in a set. Addition is the joining of two sets and discovering how many objects are altogether in both sets. Using concrete objects to demonstrate this is an important step in visualizing the process and understanding addition. To connect or link this visual representation of addition to the mathematic symbols, children should write the addition sentence that matches the picture made with the concrete objects.

What First Graders Should Know

First graders are expected to state the number sentences represented by pictures of two sets being joined together. For example, when a picture of three objects and a picture of two objects are shown, a child should be able to read the picture and state the number sentence as $3 + 2 = 5$.

Learning addition facts is an important part of the first grade curriculum, and knowing when and how to apply the addition facts is just as important. First graders are expected to learn all the addition facts up to the sum of 18. They should be able to add three numbers together ($2 + 3 + 5 = 10$), add a two-digit number to a two-digit number where no regrouping or "carrying" is required ($36 + 12 = 48$), and determine a missing addend (the numbers that are added together in an addition problem). They also should be able to write a number sentence horizontally and vertically.

Equal Sign

Explain that the equal sign (=) means that the amount on one side of the sign must be "the same as" the amount on the other side. Demonstrate this concept by drawing the equal sign on an index card and having your child put his hands on either side of the card. Put any three objects in one of his hands, and ask him to make the number of objects in both hands or on both sides of the equal sign "the same" by adding more objects. He should select three objects with his empty hand. Increase the degree of difficulty by putting an unequal number of objects in his hands and having him select enough objects with one hand so that both sides are "equal."

Sets

Make two sets with a different number of objects in each set. Read the "picture" made by the objects, and write an addition problem that matches it in horizontal form. For example, make a set with five objects and a set of two objects, read it as $5 + 2 = 7$, emphasizing the plus sign (+) and the equal sign (=), and explain that the plus sign means "added to." Arrange the sets of objects so that one is above the other, and write the same number sentence in vertical form. Point out that the numbers are written one on top of the other, the addition sign is to the left of the bottom number, and the answer does not change. The equal sign is not written as it is in the horizontal form (=), but instead, the equal sign is the line below the bottom number.

Zero Property of Addition

Using objects found in your home to make sets, demonstrate that zero plus any number will equal that number. Use word problems and have your child make the sets and join them. *Example:* Stephanie has three toys in one box and no toys in another box. How many toys does she have in all? Have your child make a set with three objects in it and a set with no objects. Have him count how many there are altogether. Lead him to discover that zero plus any number is equal to the number other than zero.

One Plus Rule

State word problems involving two sets, where one set always contains one object, and allow your child to discover that one plus any number is equal to the next higher number when counting by ones. Have your child make sets that match the numbers in a word problem and arrive at the answer by counting how many objects there are in all. Using a number line (a horizontal line with the numbers in counting order) also allows your child to explore this same concept. Describe a word problem, and have your child point to the number on the number line as it appears in the story. The word problem should include a set with one object, and your child should be adding one to the first number by pointing to the following number on the line. *Example:* Neil has three dinosaurs (your child should point to the number 3 on the number line), and his father gives him one more (the child should move his finger to the next higher number on the line, which is the 4). How many dinosaurs does Neil have now? Your child's finger should be pointing to the answer because it moved to the next higher number when a 1 was added.

Communitive Property of Addition

The communitive property of addition (order rule) states that the order in which the addends appear in an addition problem can be reversed without affecting the sum. Your child needs to understand this rule. In order to comprehend this concept, have him join two sets of objects and record the number sentence represented by the groups. Have him switch the order of the sets and record the new number sentence. For example, your child can make a set of four toys and a set of three toys and record the number sentence 4 + 3 = 7. Then he reverses the groups and has a set of three toys first and then a set of four toys and records the number sentence as 3 + 4 = 7. Since no toys were added or taken away, the answer (sum) will stay the same. After practice, have your child discover that the first addend plus the second addend will equal the second addend plus the first addend: 3 + 4 = 4 + 3.

Grouping Addition Facts

It's easier to break addition facts into small groups, which can be referred to as the "three plus facts" or the "four plus facts":

2+	3+	4+	5+	6+	7+	8+	9+
2+2	3+3	4+4	5+5	6+6	7+7	8+8	9+9
2+3	3+4	4+5	5+6	6+7	7+8	8+9	
2+4	3+5	4+6	5+7	6+8	7+9		
2+5	3+6	4+7	5+8	6+9			
2+6	3+7	4+8	5+9				
2+7	3+8	4+9					
2+8	3+9						
2+9							

"Doubles" Addition Facts

The "doubles" (any number plus itself) is the first row of the preceding chart. Children usually grasp these eight addition facts quickly.

Adding little clues like "I ate it and ate it and got 'sickteen'" may help to learn that 8 + 8 = 16.

"Doubles Plus One" Facts

Embellish the knowledge that your child has acquired by teaching the "doubles plus one." Use concrete objects to represent the doubles fact; for example, a set of three objects and another set of three objects would show 3 + 3. A "doubles plus one" fact would be 3 + 4 or [3 + (3 + 1)]. Your child should add one object to one of the sets of three in order to represent the new problem. The sum would be one more than the original problem's sum because only one object was added. Your child should verbally explain the concept by stating that since 3 + 3 = 6, 3 + 4 must equal 7 because 4 is one more than 3 and 7 is one more than 6. Understanding this concept enables your child to learn the second row of the preceding chart, leaving only 21 facts to learn.

The Nine Plus Rule

Teaching the nine plus rule through the use of objects and making sets of 10 will allow your child to learn the nine plus number facts without memorizing them. In order to teach 9 + 5, make a set of 9 objects and another set of 5 objects. Take one object from the set of 5 leaving 4, and move it to the set of 9 to make it a set of 10. Now you have 1 ten and 4 ones, or 14. Try another problem: 9 + 7. Make a set of 9 objects and a set of 7 objects. Take one object from the set of 7, leaving 6, and move it to the set of 9 to make it a set of 10. Now you have 1 ten and 6 ones, or 16. Lead to the generalization that the sum of a nine plus addition fact will have a one in the tens place, and the number in the ones place will be one less than the addend other than the nine. After your child understands this concept, he will only need to memorize 15 facts!

Counting On

In order to add two sets of objects using the "counting on" method, your child needs to select the higher number in a given addition number sentence and count from that number as many times as the other addend states. For example, in the number sentence 5 + 2, your child should select the higher number (obviously, 5), state it (5), and count up two numbers (6, 7). This strategy is very useful learning the remaining plus two facts. If your child is using this strategy to add greater numbers, he can state the higher number in the addition sentence and then draw dots on a piece of paper to match the lesser addend. He should count as he points to each of the dots. For example, in the number sentence 3 + 5, your child should state 5 and make 3 dots. He should count 5, 6, 7, 8. If your child can grasp the aforementioned addition strategies, he only needs to memorize 10 addition facts. These 10 facts are underlined in the preceding chart that shows how to group the addition facts. Strategies should be learned using concrete objects linking meaning to the number facts. You can help your child memorize the remaining facts by attaching clues to them; for example, singing "four plus seven is e-le-ven" helps to remember 4 + 7 = 11.

Adding Three Numbers

Using three sets of objects, write the numbers represented by these sets, and choose two of the numbers to add together first. Draw lines that meet from these two numbers, and write their sum next to them. Now add that sum to the third addend. Count the objects, and check to see if that number matches the sum that was written.

Adding a Two-Digit Number to a Two-Digit Number

Even though these problems do not require regrouping or "carrying" in first grade, emphasize to your child that the ones column will always be the starting point in any addition problem. Then he is to add the numbers in the tens column. This approach to addition will instill good math habits.

Have your child use bundles of straws and single straws to show the addition problem. When your child adds, say, 27 + 52, he should show the number 27 with 2 bundles of ten and 7 ones, and he should show the number 52 with 5 bundles of ten and 2 ones. When he adds them or joins them together, he will have 7 bundles of ten and 9 ones, or 79. This should match the sum he has in written form.

What You and Your Child Can Do

In order for your child to connect meaning to the addition facts and explore the process of addition, you should relate the process to objects in your child's environment. Children have already been exposed to addition informally in various situations. Children are natural collectors; whether it is dolls, figurines, stamps, coins, or butterflies, when they engage in collecting things, they are really joining sets or adding when they realize how many they have in total. Children need to connect this knowledge with the mathematic symbols. Here are some ways to help your child learn about the concept of addition:

Using brief stories or word problems, have your child use concrete objects and make sets to match the numbers in your story. For example, your story may state that Nancy has four balloons and Larry has three, how many do they have in all? Your child may use any objects to represent the balloons and make a set of four and a set of three using those objects. Then he should count the total number of objects to arrive at the answer. Practice telling many different story problems that involve joining two sets together.

Missing Addend. Show a particular number of pennies, stones, or other small items. Start with a low number of items, and add more as your child gains confidence with this activity. Have your child hide his eyes while you divide the items into two sets, one in each hand. Open one hand and display the number of items in it. Have your child write the number sentence using a blank where the missing addend would appear and determine how many items are in your closed hand.

Your child must decide how many more items—in addition to the ones he sees in the open hand—are needed to equal the total he saw before he closed his eyes. Have him verify his answer by checking the hidden items and then filling in the blank in the number sentence. Example: Put six pennies on the table. Have your child look at the six pennies and then hide his eyes. Pick up two pennies in one hand and four in the other. Have your child open his eyes, and then show him the four pennies in your one opened hand. Keep your other hand closed. He should write the number sentence as 4 + __ = 6 to match the information he knows. Now he needs to determine how many pennies must be in the closed hand to equal a total of six pennies. He can use the "counting on" method to discover the answer and then write it in the blank as 4 + 2 = 6.

"High or Low." Play "High or Low" with a regular deck of playing cards minus the tens and face cards. Deal each player two cards that are placed face down and one card that is face up; the dealer also takes three cards but doesn't show them. Take turns being the dealer. The players predict if the sum of their cards will be higher or lower than the dealer's three cards. Turn over the cards and add all three cards together. If the prediction is correct, the player gets a point. If the prediction is incorrect, the dealer gets the point. If it is a tie, the dealer gets the point. The one with the most points is the winner.

"War" with Dice. This game is played with two players, using two dice and a paper plate for each player and markers such as beans, Cheerios, or minimarshmallows. When the word

ADDITION

war is said, both players roll their dice on their plates and add up the numbers on the dice. Whoever has the higher sum gets a marker. Continue playing until one player reaches 10 markers. You may use regular dice, but polyhedra (many sided) dice are available at education stores. There are dice with the numbers from one to nine, and these are the ideal dice to use when practicing all the addition facts.

"Come My Way." Create a playing board by drawing a center starting space and 10 blank spaces on both sides of the center. Have one player sit with the 10 blank spaces facing toward him and the opponent sit with the other 10 blank spaces facing him. Place one marker on the center space, and use addition flashcards showing addition facts that need to be practiced. Decide who goes first. The first player turns over a flashcard, answers the problem, and moves the marker toward him the number of spaces that are in the ones column of the sum. Take turns turning over a flashcard, answering the problem, and moving the same marker toward the player who is answering the addition problem. The marker will move back and forth along the board. The first one to move the marker off his side of the board is declared the winner of "Come My Way!"

"Guess My Number." Three players and a regular deck of playing cards (minus the face cards and the tens) are needed to play this game. Of the three people, one person is designated the dealer and the sum caller, and this person is not dealt any cards. The dealer gives one card to each player. Without looking, the two players place their card to their foreheads so that they cannot see their own card but are able to see their opponent's card. The dealer looks at the cards of both players and calls out the sum of the two numbers on the cards. The first player to guess his own number gets the point. In order to guess it, the player must determine what the missing addend is. He must think: "What (my number) plus my opponent's number equals the sum that the dealer called out?"

Make an Addition Book. Read Keith Baker's *Quack and Count* book that shows all the different combinations of numbers that have the sum of seven. This cute, short book uses ducks to illustrate different addition number sentences. Help your child make your own "Quack and Count" book illustrating all the different ways to make the sum of another number.

What Tests May Ask

One- and two-digit addition is a math computation skill and is included in that portion of the test. Your child will be asked simply to solve the problems in a certain amount of time and probably to solve some word problems involving one- and two-digit numerals. Children may be expected to choose correct number sentences to match pictures, choose correct math signs, fill in the missing addends, and correctly solve one-, two-, and three-digit addition problems (both vertically and horizontally) with no regrouping.

Practice Skill: Addition

Directions: Listen carefully to the following questions, and darken in the bubble beside the correct answer.

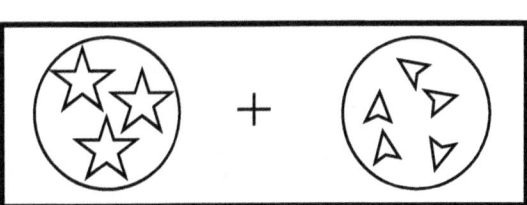

Example:

What number sentence matches this picture?

Ⓐ $2 + 1 = 3$ Ⓑ $3 + 5 = 8$

Ⓒ $2 + 5 = 7$ Ⓓ $3 + 3 = 6$

Answer:

Ⓑ $3 + 5 = 8$

1 Which sign means "plus"?
- Ⓐ =
- Ⓑ +
- Ⓒ –
- Ⓓ /

2 What number sentence matches this picture?
- Ⓐ 3 + 3 = 6
- Ⓑ 6 – 3 = 3
- Ⓒ 6 + 3 = 9
- Ⓓ 6 + 4 = 10

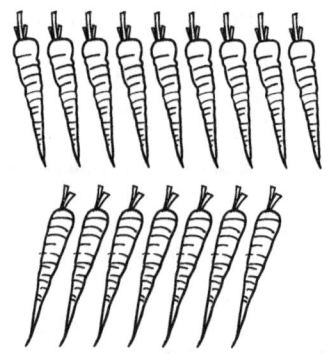

3 What number sentence matches this picture?
- Ⓐ 8 + 7 = 15
- Ⓑ 9 – 7 = 2
- Ⓒ 9 + 6 = 15
- Ⓓ 9 + 7 = 16

4 Fill in the blank. 9 __ 6 = 15
- Ⓐ +
- Ⓑ –
- Ⓒ =
- Ⓓ /

Directions: Look at these math problems and select the correct answers.

Example:

3 + 3 = __
- Ⓐ 3
- Ⓑ 6
- Ⓒ 5
- Ⓓ 0

Answer:
- Ⓑ 6

5 5 + 2 = __
- Ⓐ 5
- Ⓑ 52
- Ⓒ 3
- Ⓓ 7

ADDITION

6 6 + 5 = __
- Ⓐ 9
- Ⓑ 1
- Ⓒ 11
- Ⓓ 65

7 0 + 7 = __
- Ⓐ 70
- Ⓑ 7
- Ⓒ 0
- Ⓓ 8

8 7 + 9 = __
- Ⓐ 79
- Ⓑ 2
- Ⓒ 16
- Ⓓ 18

9 5
   + 4
- Ⓐ 6
- Ⓑ 1
- Ⓒ 9
- Ⓓ 8

10 8
    + 4
- Ⓐ 13
- Ⓑ 3
- Ⓒ 12
- Ⓓ 15

11 6
    + 6
- Ⓐ 60
- Ⓑ 0
- Ⓒ 12
- Ⓓ 14

12 3
    + 9
- Ⓐ 12
- Ⓑ 13
- Ⓒ 10
- Ⓓ 6

13 Fill in the missing addend:
7 + __ = 12.
- Ⓐ 5
- Ⓑ 19
- Ⓒ 9
- Ⓓ 4

14 Fill in the missing addend:
2 + __ = 5.
- Ⓐ 2
- Ⓑ 4
- Ⓒ 3
- Ⓓ 7

15 5 + 1 + 3 = __
- Ⓐ 12
- Ⓑ 9
- Ⓒ 7
- Ⓓ 10

16 0 + 4 + 6 = __
- Ⓐ 8
- Ⓑ 9
- Ⓒ 10
- Ⓓ 11

17 44
     + 23
- Ⓐ 21
- Ⓑ 67
- Ⓒ 76
- Ⓓ 27

18 21
     + 35
- Ⓐ 12
- Ⓑ 55
- Ⓒ 58
- Ⓓ 56

19 3
      4
     + 1
- Ⓐ 7
- Ⓑ 6
- Ⓒ 5
- Ⓓ 8

ADDITION

20
```
  5
  2
+ 7
```
Ⓐ 14
Ⓑ 12
Ⓒ 13
Ⓓ 10

21 4 + 2 + 5 = __
Ⓐ 10
Ⓑ 11
Ⓒ 12
Ⓓ 9

22 3 + 1 + 4 = __
Ⓐ 5
Ⓑ 6
Ⓒ 7
Ⓓ 8

23
```
  57
+  2
```
Ⓐ 79
Ⓑ 55
Ⓒ 59
Ⓓ 50

24
```
  34
+  5
```
Ⓐ 39
Ⓑ 30
Ⓒ 31
Ⓓ 89

25 12 + 6 = __
Ⓐ 6
Ⓑ 17
Ⓒ 24
Ⓓ 18

(See page 103 for answer key.)

CHAPTER 4

Subtraction

Subtraction is the inverse of addition. It is taking away some objects from a set and discovering how many objects remain. Subtraction is also used to compare two sets to determine the difference in the number of objects between the sets. In order to do this, the number of objects in the smaller set (the number where the sets are equal) is subtracted from the number of objects in the larger set. The objects remaining will be the difference between the two sets.

What First Graders Should Know

Subtraction is harder for children to master than addition. First graders are expected to be able to translate into mathematic symbols a picture showing a subtraction story. They are learning how to relate their knowledge about addition to subtraction through a concept referred to as the *family of facts*.

This concept relates four number sentences, two subtraction and two addition. An example of the family of facts is as follows: Since 4 + 3 = 7 and 3 + 4 = 7, then 7 − 3 = 4 and 7 − 4 = 3. Children are expected to use strategies for subtraction to answer problems.

In addition to the family-of-facts strategy, they learn how to draw circles to represent the numbers in the number sentence, and they cross off the number of circles that are to be subtracted in the problem. The pattern of minus 0 and minus 1 and the "count back" strategies are also used to help children learn to subtract. First graders are also expected to be able to subtract a one-digit number or a two-digit number from a two-digit number when no regrouping, or "borrowing," is required. Writing a subtraction problem in vertical and horizontal form is also a first grade skill.

Subtracting from a Two-Digit Number

Showing your child objects that represent a two-digit number, ask her to subtract a specific number of objects. Make sure that no regrouping, or "borrowing," is required; borrowing is introduced in second grade. Have your child record the number sentence in vertical form and subtract in the ones column first and then proceed to the tens column. Remind her that this is the same procedure that is used in addition, but this time you subtract the numbers in both columns. Emphasize that the bottom number is subtracted from the top number, and if the top is not greater, the bottom number must be subtracted from the whole number. For example, in the problem

$$\begin{array}{r} 14 \\ -6 \\ \hline \end{array}$$

you can't say "4 minus 6," you must say "14 minus 6."

A very common mistake is made soon after a child learns to subtract a two-digit number from a two-digit number. Incorrect answers such as the following are made often: 14 − 5 = 11. The child has attempted to subtract 5 from 4 in the ones column and has arrived at the incorrect answer of 1, when in reality, 5 from 4 requires the child to use the whole number, 14. Remind your child to check to make sure that the top number is greater than the bottom number so that she can accurately subtract. Use concrete objects to demonstrate that she can't take 5 ones away from the 4 ones. She must use the entire top number. Explain that in the process of addition, the addends may be changed around without affecting the answer; however, in subtraction, the greater number must be first.

What You and Your Child Can Do

The Snack Muncher. Begin the concept of subtraction using concrete objects. Tell stories that will translate into a subtraction problem. Eating snacks creates a wonderful opportunity to relate real objects to subtraction. If your child has five pieces of candy and eats three, make the appropriate subtraction number sentence and write it for your child, emphasizing the "minus" sign (−). Explain that it means "minus" or "take away." After repeated practice, allow your child to write the subtraction number sentence independently.

Read My Picture. Draw pictures of subtraction stories. You may want to draw four ducks in the water and two waddling away. Relate this to the number sentence 6 (total number of ducks) − 2 (2 going away) = (equals) 4 (ducks left in the water).

Minus Zero. Using concrete objects, demonstrate that taking zero items away from any set does not change the original set.

Minus One. Explain that whenever one is taken away from any given number, the answer simply will be one less than that original number. Use concrete objects to demonstrate this concept, and allow your child to verify her answer by counting the objects left in the set after one object has been removed. Writing the number sentence after she has been given a chance to visualize it is helpful in relating the concrete stage (manipulating the objects) to the abstract stage (using the mathematical symbols).

Count Back. Starting with about ten objects, arrange them in a horizontal line. Have your child count the number of objects aloud. Cover the last one with a piece of paper, and have your child discover how many are left. Cover another object, and have your child "count back" another number every time another object is covered. You may practice again using fewer or more objects, depending on how difficult this activity is for your child. If she reaches a point whereby she isn't able to count backwards from memory, allow her to count the objects and start again. Practice using the number line (a piece of paper with the numbers 1 to 20 written on it) is also a valuable tool when using the "count back" method. Given a subtraction number sentence, find the first number in the number sentence on the number line, and count backwards the number of spaces equaling the number being subtracted. The answer will be the number on which you land after counting backwards.

Crossing Out. Use word problems and allow your child to draw circles to represent the objects in the story. After you have told her how many objects are leaving or being taken away, have her "cross out" that many objects and count the remaining objects to arrive at the answer. Record her answer in a complete number sentence.

Family of Facts. Have your child draw a house with two windows and two doors. On the windows show two related addition number sentences (addition sentences with the numbers in different order, for example, 6 + 7 = 13 and 7 + 6 = 13), and on the doors show the two subtraction number sentences (13 − 7 = 6 and 13 − 6 = 7).

SUBTRACTION

Lead your child to relate subtraction and addition when presented with a subtraction problem such as 13 − 6, by asking herself the question: What number plus the 6 equals 13?

Candy Blocks. Using two different colored blocks or pieces of candy also can help your child to see how addition and subtraction are related. Arrange six red blocks and three blue blocks together. Your child should be able to describe the addition number sentences related to this picture as 6 + 3 = 9 and 3 + 6 = 9. Ask her to state the subtraction number sentence of this picture if, for instance, the six red blocks were removed. She should be able to state 9 (altogether) − 6 = 3. Now ask her to describe the subtraction number sentence when the three blue blocks are separated from the set.

She should state 9 (altogether) − 3 = 6. Repeated practice with objects will help your child grasp the family of facts concept.

What's the Difference? Using a deck of regular playing cards, remove the tens and face cards, and deal four cards to each player. Each player looks at her cards and arranges them so that the two highest cards are on top and the two lowest cards are underneath them, making two two-digit numbers. Each player subtracts the number she has made with the bottom cards from the number she has made with the top cards. Whoever has the highest difference is the winner. For example, if a 2, 4, 7, and 6 were dealt, they should be arranged in the following order:

$$\begin{array}{r} 76 \\ -42 \\ \hline \end{array}$$

The difference is 34

You may increase the level of difficulty of this game and really challenge your child by changing the rules. For example, you may arrange the cards in the order that you think will allow you to have the greatest difference. The same cards that were dealt above could be arranged in many ways:

$$\begin{array}{r} 74 \\ -62 \\ \hline \end{array} \quad \begin{array}{r} 76 \\ -24 \\ \hline \end{array} \quad \begin{array}{r} 67 \\ -24 \\ \hline \end{array} \quad \begin{array}{r} 76 \\ -42 \\ \hline \end{array}$$

You may use the same game to find the lowest difference. Games such as this are as entertaining as they are challenging!

Cover Up. Using two dice, plus items to mark a space and two pieces of paper with the numerals 1 through 12 on them, give each player one of the papers. The object of the game is to have the most numbers covered. Take turns rolling the dice. The player who rolls the dice may either add the numbers on the dice or subtract them and then cover the sum or difference. For example, if a 3 and a 4 are rolled, the player can cover either a 1 or a 7. If both numbers are covered, she is not able to cover any number, and possession of the dice goes to her opponent. When the playing time is over, the player who has the lowest sum when all the uncovered numbers are added together is the winner.

Subtraction Race. Make a board game with a path of squares to get from a starting point to a finishing point. Using two dodecahedron dice (twelve-sided dice available at educational stores for a minimal cost), take turns rolling the dice and subtracting the smaller number from the higher number. The player may move as many spaces as the difference between the numbers she rolled. The first player to the finish point is the winner. Six-sided dice may be substituted for the dodecahedron dice when the game is intended for children who are just learning to subtract.

Computer Fun. Computer games such as *Franklin Learns Math* and *Number Munchers* provide motivation while practicing subtraction facts. They are appropriately geared for first grade children.

What Tests May Ask

Standardized tests in first grade will assess a child's ability to read a subtraction picture and match a number sentence with it and subtract vertical and horizontal subtraction problems. These tests also will assess a child's ability to subtract a one-digit number or a two-digit number from a two-digit number when no regrouping, or "borrowing," is required.

Practice Skill: Subtraction

Directions: Listen carefully to each question, and darken in the bubble beside the correct answer.

Example:

Which number sentence matches the picture?

- Ⓐ 5 − 2 = 3
- Ⓑ 7 − 2 = 5
- Ⓒ 2 − 7 = 5
- Ⓓ 6 − 2 = 4

Answer:

- Ⓑ 7 − 2 = 5

1 Which number sentence matches the picture above?
- Ⓐ 1 + 4 = 5
- Ⓑ 5 − 1 = 4
- Ⓒ 4 − 1 = 3
- Ⓓ 4 − 3 = 1

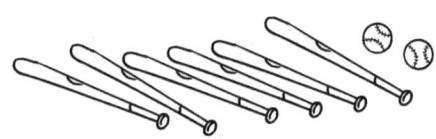

2 How many more bats than balls are there? Find the number sentence that matches the picture.
- Ⓐ 6 + 2 = 8
- Ⓑ 5 + 2 = 7
- Ⓒ 6 − 2 = 4
- Ⓓ 2 + 2 = 4

SUBTRACTION

3 How many fewer books are there than pencils? Find the number sentence that matches the picture.

Ⓐ 8 − 3 = 5
Ⓑ 8 + 3 = 11
Ⓒ 7 − 3 = 4
Ⓓ 8 − 3 = 6

○○○○○○✕✕

4 What number sentence does the picture show?

Ⓐ 6 + 2 = 8
Ⓑ 8 − 2 = 6
Ⓓ 8 + 2 = 10
Ⓓ 6 − 2 = 4

5 12 __ 5 = 7

Ⓐ +
Ⓑ −
Ⓒ =
Ⓓ /

6 7 − 4 = __

Ⓐ 2
Ⓑ 3
Ⓒ 4
Ⓓ 1

7 26 − 10 = __

Ⓐ 36
Ⓑ 9
Ⓒ 16
Ⓓ 61

8 24
   − 12

Ⓐ 36
Ⓑ 12
Ⓒ 16
Ⓓ 11

9 18
   − 9

Ⓐ 11
Ⓑ 8
Ⓒ 9
Ⓓ 10

37

10 12
    − 7
- Ⓐ 19
- Ⓑ 15
- Ⓒ 5
- Ⓓ 8

11 15
    − 8
- Ⓐ 13
- Ⓑ 7
- Ⓒ 8
- Ⓓ 6

12 49
    − 26
- Ⓐ 63
- Ⓑ 615
- Ⓒ 23
- Ⓓ 25

13 14 − 7 = __
- Ⓐ 6
- Ⓑ 7
- Ⓒ 8
- Ⓓ 21

14 10 − 6 = __
- Ⓐ 3
- Ⓑ 16
- Ⓒ 4
- Ⓓ 5

15 16 − 8 = __
- Ⓐ 12
- Ⓑ 24
- Ⓒ 9
- Ⓓ 8

(See page 103 for answer key.)

CHAPTER 5

Time: Clocks and Calendars

Telling Time

Since the use of digital clocks and digital watches has become commonplace, children have little opportunity to practice telling time on an analog clock (a clock with a circular face and hands). Many homes don't contain any clocks with hour and minute hands, which means that children aren't familiar with this method of telling time.

What First Graders Should Know

Children in first grade are taught how to tell time to the hour and to the half hour. Given repeated practice with telling time to the hour on an analog clock, and distinguishing the difference between the hour hand and the minute hand, most children this age are able to master this concept. Still, even late first graders may have some lingering problems with telling time, even if the clocks have very large numbers. Most children this age will be confused with clocks featuring Roman numerals.

However, many children have problems telling time to the half hour. The most common mistake children make is naming the incorrect hour. You should be careful to name the hour that the hour hand has passed. Often, children will state the hour that the hour hand is approaching; for example, when the clock is set at 4:30, a child often states the incorrect time as 5:30.

A child's first experience with the concept of time usually involves bedtime, a specific time a daily activity occurs, or a particular time a favorite TV program starts. Associating the time shown on the clock with these real-life situations will help your child become familiar with telling time. It also will help motivate your child to learn to tell time and make the concept of time become more meaningful. Here's how to help:

1. Explain that the minute hand is longer than the hour hand and that it is used to calculate minutes. Your child should understand that the numbers written on the face of the clock represent hours and that the hour hand points to the specific hour. Some children may confuse the hour and the minute hands.

2. Explain that the markings between the numbers stand for minutes and that there are five minutes from one number to the next.

3. Show how the hands work simultaneously: The hour hand moves from one number to the next while the minute hand moves from the 12 completely around the clock until it reaches 12 again.

4. Practice telling time on an analog clock that is set at different times to the hour.

5. Practice counting by fives as you point to each number on the clock emphasizing the minutes. Provide lots of practice with telling time to the half hour.

6. Provide a mixed practice: telling time to the hour and half hour.

7. Practice writing the time in two different ways: in symbol form (12:00 or 12:30) and in written form (12 o'clock and 12 thirty, or thirty minutes past 12).

8. Explain that the numbers before the colon on a digital clock represent the hours and that the numbers after the colon represent the number of minutes it is past the hour.

What You and Your Child Can Do

The Grouchy Ladybug. This book by Eric Carle reinforces the concept of telling time with an analog clock. Children love it!

Make a Clock. Help your child make a clock using a bendable brass fastener, two pieces of construction paper for the hour and minute hands, and a paper plate.

1. Trace the hour and minute hands on the construction paper.
2. Let your child cut them out.
3. Punch a center hole in the paper plate and a hole at the end of each "hand."
4. Let your child print the numbers on the paper plate clock "face."
5. Push the brass fastener through the holes in the ends of the clock hands and through the center of the plate; bend the fastener behind the plate to fasten.
6. Have your child rotate the hands to make different hour and half-hour times on the clock.

Make a Picture. Let your child pick his favorite time of the day to the half hour. Have him draw a clock depicting that time. Then, beneath the clock picture, have him draw a picture of what he is doing at that time.

Just a Minute... Ask your child to make up some activities that take less than a minute to complete. This helps reinforce how long a "minute" really is.

TV Times. Have your child come up with a few favorite TV programs that are a half hour long. Let him check the clock before and after the program to see the clock display the hour and half-hour times.

What Tests May Ask

Standardized tests for this age assess the ability to tell time in two ways. First, they will present pictures of clocks and ask children to choose the correct time from a choice of answers. Second, the tests include questions on elapsed time. The test will give a time when an activity begins and when it stops, asking the child to figure out how much time has elapsed in between.

Practice Skill: Telling Time

Directions: Listen carefully to the question, and darken in the bubble beside the correct answer.

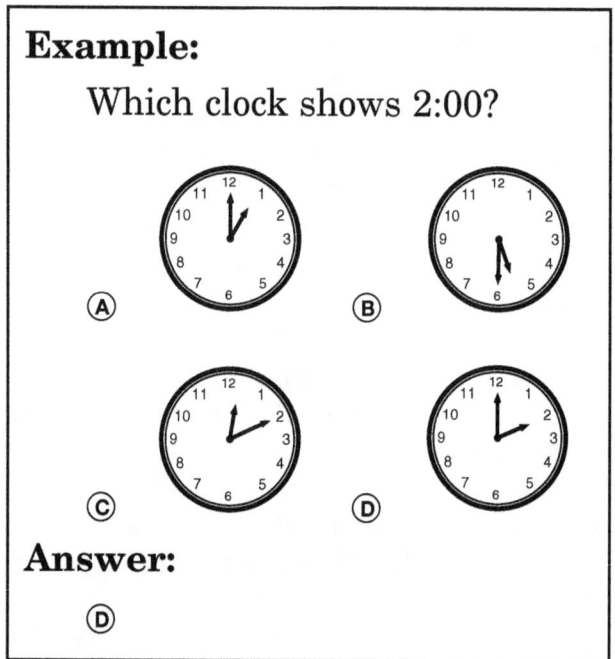

TIME: CLOCKS AND CALENDARS

1 Which clock shows 3:00?

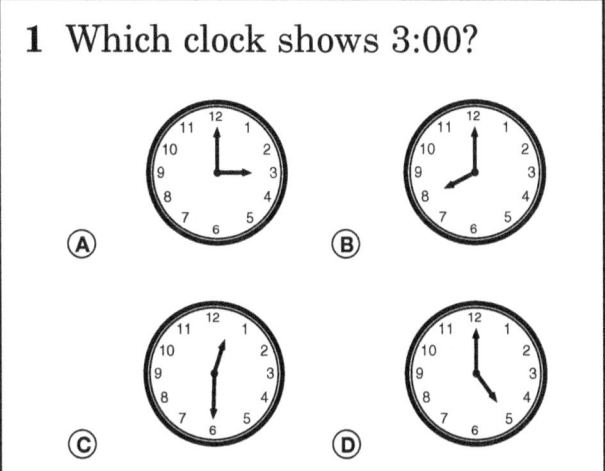

2 Which clock shows 5:30?

3 Which clock shows thirty minutes after 12?

4 My favorite TV show starts at 4:30 p.m. and is one half hour long. What time is it over?

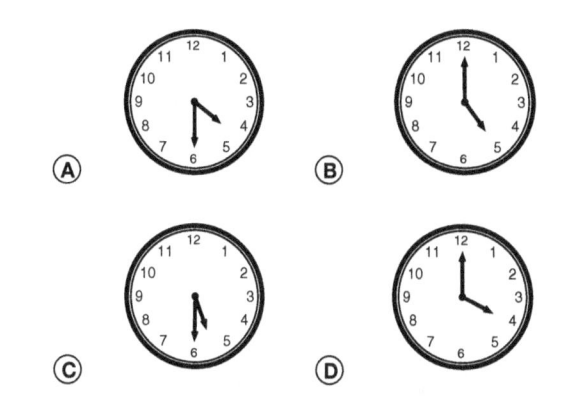

5 What time is it on this clock?

- Ⓐ 1:00
- Ⓑ 10:00
- Ⓒ 10:30
- Ⓓ 11:00

6 What time is it?

- Ⓐ 7:00
- Ⓑ 8:30
- Ⓒ 7:30
- Ⓓ 6:30

(See page 103 for answer key.)

Calendars

Knowing how to read and decode a calendar is becoming a crucial skill at a younger and younger age—even for first graders! While most classrooms make the daily calendar an important beginning for the day, there is a lot to learn about the passage of time. Time also includes calendar concepts. First-grade children are expected to identify and place in order the days of the week and the months of the year and decipher information about a particular month on a calendar.

What First Graders Should Know

Don't despair if, at the beginning of the year, your child is struggling with the names of the months, days of the week, and the order in which they come. Most young first graders won't be able to locate the months just by looking through the calendar. However, by the end of first grade, most children can use a calendar confidently, locating dates you ask them for or identifying the date if you point to it.

What You and Your Child Can Do

Personal Calendar. Provide your child with his own calendar so that he can become familiar with the days of the week and dates of the month—either buy a calendar or make one on a computer. Let your child decorate it as he wishes—the key is to get him to use it. Allow him to draw pictures of activities or holidays that will occur on various dates within the month. Using the calendar, help your child find his birthday month, and record how many days are in that month and how many Sundays, Tuesdays, and so on are included in the month.

Color the Days. Using a calendar, have your child select one month and color all the Saturdays red, all the Tuesdays blue, and so on. Have your child discover the pattern that the days of the week are listed in a column.

Let's Sing. Have your child sing the days of the week to you in order. Have him discover the number of days in a week.

Let's Make a Diary. Let your child make a diary by having him create a booklet with a calendar showing the days of the week. Have him draw pictures of what he does on special days.

What Tests May Ask

You can be fairly certain that most standardized tests will include some questions about calendars, asking specific questions designed to assess a child's ability to understand names of the months, days of the week, and dates. Tests may show a picture of a calendar and ask specific questions about that calendar in a variety of ways.

Practice Skill: Calendars

Directions: Look at the calendar that follows to answer questions 7 through 11.

TIME: CLOCKS AND CALENDARS

DECEMBER 2000

Sunday	Monday	Tuesday	Wednesday	Thursday	Friday	Saturday
					1	2
3	4	5	6	7	8	9
10	11	12	13	14	15	16
17	18	19	20	21	22	23
24/31	25	26	27	28	29	30

Example:

What day of the week comes right after Tuesday?

- Ⓐ Monday
- Ⓑ Wednesday
- Ⓒ Friday
- Ⓓ Saturday

Answer:

- Ⓑ Wednesday

7 What day of the week comes right before Tuesday?

- Ⓐ Monday
- Ⓑ Wednesday
- Ⓒ Saturday
- Ⓓ Sunday

8 What day of the week is December 16?

- Ⓐ Sunday
- Ⓑ Wednesday
- Ⓒ Saturday
- Ⓓ Monday

9 How many days are in December?

- Ⓐ 31
- Ⓑ 12
- Ⓒ 13
- Ⓓ 25

10 How many days are in one week?

- Ⓐ 5
- Ⓑ 7
- Ⓒ 14
- Ⓓ 30

11 On December 19, Betsy's mother reminded her that she has an appointment with her doctor next Wednesday. What date of the month is her doctor visit?

- Ⓐ 27
- Ⓑ 13
- Ⓒ 20
- Ⓓ 29

(See page 103 for answer key.)

CHAPTER 6

Money

Teaching a child to count money can be a challenging task, but when all the prerequisite skills are met in a sequential manner, a great deal of frustration can be avoided. Various skills are necessary to count money, and each step along the hierarchy needs to be learned in order to count money successfully. Money concepts should be taught on the very first day of school and continued throughout the school year—not just as an isolated unit. Instruction should begin simply—and concepts should not be rushed!

What First Graders Should Know

Children in first grade are expected to be able to count pennies, nickels, dimes, and quarters to an amount that doesn't exceed one dollar. They also should know the names and values of each of the coins.

Children are taught to match a group of coins to a specific amount. Confusion often arises when identifying the values of a nickel and a dime, however, because the larger coin (the nickel) is worth less than the smaller coin (the dime). This doesn't coincide with their predictions. Many children know the value of a penny, and verifying that a penny is also larger than a dime helps to make children more confident that the dime is also worth more than the nickel.

Many first graders have trouble when asked to add dimes to an amount that ends with a 5. Children may find it easier to add two multiples of 5 to the amount rather than adding a 10.

Besides counting coins, first graders also learn how to determine how much money they will have left if an item is purchased for a certain price when they are presented with a group of coins. In order to do this, children need to learn the strategy of crossing out the number of coins that equal the price of the item and then counting the remaining coins.

Counting Money

Here are the steps involved in teaching your child how to count money:

1. Identify the coins by name: penny, nickel, dime, and quarter. Be sure to include identifying the coin by the "heads" side of the coin as well as the "tails" side.

2. Match the coins to the value they represent.

3. Arrange different coins in order from the largest value to the smallest value.

4. Count by ones, fives, tens, and twenty-fives. Counting by twenty-fives is needed to count quarters but is rarely practiced or recognized as a necessary skill.

5. Count all coins of one denomination first. Start with counting all pennies. Proceed to counting all nickels, then all dimes, and finally all quarters.

6. Learn to add multiples of 10 to numbers that end in a 5.

7. Count coins with different values. Begin by counting two different coins. Have your child arrange coins in order from the larger value to the smaller value. Count aloud

saying the value up to that point as the child touches each coin (Example: Three dimes and then five pennies. 10, 20, 30, 31, 32, 33, 34, 35.) Continue counting two different coins until all possibilities are completed.

8. Count coins with three different values. Arrange the coins in order from the highest value to the lowest value in a line from left to right. Count aloud saying the value up to that point as each coin is touched. The last number stated is the total amount. Continue counting three different coins until all possibilities are reached.

9. Practice counting different amounts with all four coins.

What You and Your Child Can Do

All the activities below will provide your child with practice naming and counting coins and learning the value of coins—while providing fun and excitement. Using real money is suggested to provide a realistic scenario.

Pocket Change. Allow your child to count the change in your pocketbook or in your pocket. (You may want to let your child add the change to her piggy bank!)

Memory Game. Practice naming the coins by playing a memory game. Place all four coins on a tray. Have your child hide her eyes while you remove one of the coins. The child looks at the remaining coins and names the one you've removed.

Grocery Store. Save your empty Jell-O boxes, egg cartons, and snack and cereal boxes. Assign unrealistically low prices to the items, and allow your child to use coins to match the prices and "buy" the items one at a time. Small paper bags, toy grocery carts, and a toy cash register add to the fun.

Bakery. Shape soft clay into bakery items, and attach prices to the "baked goods." Take turns being the cashier and the customer. Coin purses or wallets and real money can add excitement to the game. Sorry, no credit cards allowed!

Book Store. Here's a fun game using your child's books. Attach unrealistically low prices to the books using reusable labels and play "Bookstore" by buying one book at a time. The customer also can place all her money on the table and count out the price of the book, pay the cashier, and finally, count all the money she has left.

Read! Try reading Judith Viorst's *Alexander, Who Used to Be Rich Last Sunday* to your child, and have her use the same coins that the main character (Alexander) uses. Have your child lose his money, as Alexander does, while you read the story.

Shop Right. When you are at the store, allow your child to pay the cashier and receive the change for one item that you buy for her.

What Tests May Ask

Only a few pages of most standardized tests are devoted to money, for a total of about five to ten questions. Most of these will ask students to identify a set of coins that equals the amount shown, choose the amount that is represented by the picture shown, or choose an alternate way to make a given amount. Tests may include word problems, and one or two may ask about making change. Some tabulations will need to be done on scratch paper and then transferred to the test page.

Practice Skill: Money

Directions: Look at the pictures in the following problems. Listen carefully to each question. Then darken in the bubble beside the correct answer.

MONEY

Example:

Choose the value of this coin.

- Ⓐ 5 cents
- Ⓑ 25 cents
- Ⓒ 10 cents
- Ⓓ 50 cents

Answer:

- Ⓑ 25 cents

1. Look at this picture. Which coin is worth more than 3 cents but less than 9 cents?
   - Ⓐ nickel
   - Ⓑ dime
   - Ⓒ quarter
   - Ⓓ none of the above

2. Name the coin pictured here.
   - Ⓐ nickel
   - Ⓑ quarter
   - Ⓒ dime
   - Ⓓ none of the above

3. Name the coin pictured here.
   - Ⓐ penny
   - Ⓑ nickel
   - Ⓒ dime
   - Ⓓ none of the above

4. Write the amount shown here.
   - Ⓐ 15 cents
   - Ⓑ 30 cents
   - Ⓒ 3 cents
   - Ⓓ 40 cents

5 Write the amount shown here.
- Ⓐ 31 cents
- Ⓑ 16 cents
- Ⓒ 26 cents
- Ⓓ 20 cents

6 How many pennies equal the coin shown here?
- Ⓐ 25
- Ⓑ 15
- Ⓒ 10
- Ⓓ 5

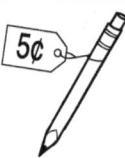

7 Look at the picture. How much will three pencils cost?
- Ⓐ 10 cents
- Ⓑ 20 cents
- Ⓒ 15 cents
- Ⓓ 30 cents

8 Mary has one quarter, and she finds two dimes. How much does she have now?
- Ⓐ 35 cents
- Ⓑ 15 cents
- Ⓒ 40 cents
- Ⓓ 45 cents

9 Neil bought a bat for 10 cents and a ball for 6 cents. How much money did he spend in all?
- Ⓐ 12 cents
- Ⓑ 4 cents
- Ⓒ 16 cents
- Ⓓ 26 cents

10 Sally had 12 cents and lost 4 cents. How much money does she have now?
- Ⓐ 8 cents
- Ⓑ 16 cents
- Ⓒ 7 cents
- Ⓓ 9 cents

11 Joe has a dime and a nickel. He gave his dad 7 cents. How much does he have now?
- Ⓐ 6 cents
- Ⓑ 8 cents
- Ⓒ 15 cents
- Ⓓ 17 cents

MONEY

12 Stephanie has 12 cents. She wants to buy a CD for 18 cents. How much more money does she need?

- Ⓐ 10 cents
- Ⓑ 8 cents
- Ⓒ 6 cents
- Ⓓ 12 cents

13 Cheryl uses two quarters to pay for a doll. She gets 20 cents change. How much did the doll cost?

- Ⓐ 30 cents
- Ⓑ 20 cents
- Ⓒ 50 cents
- Ⓓ 3 cents

(See page 103 for answer key.)

CHAPTER 7

Geometry

You may be surprised to hear that your child is studying geometry in first grade, but these days the study of shapes begins very early. Geometry in first grade focuses on learning about certain two-dimensional and three-dimensional shapes.

Children are exposed to shapes at very early ages. Many toys intended for the years of infancy are made of different solid (three-dimensional) shapes that even babies can explore. Beyond infancy, the intended purpose of some toys available for young children is to have the children sort objects by shape or to have them match shapes with their corresponding openings.

What First Graders Should Know

First graders are asked to identify shapes by name, describe them, and relate shapes to objects in their environment. They are expected to differentiate between (and describe) the following two-dimensional shapes: circles, squares, rectangles, and triangles. They are also exposed to the following three-dimensional shapes: cubes, spheres, pyramids, cylinders, cones, and rectangular prisms (boxes).

Finding objects that resemble these shapes in the world around them is also a first grade expectation. In order to do this, the children must be able to explore the objects by examining them and recognize how the shapes are alike and how they are different.

The concept of symmetry (both portions of the shape match when it is divided in half) is introduced at this age, and children are expected to determine whether or not certain shapes are symmetrical.

What You and Your Child Can Do

Two-Dimensional Shapes

Circles, rectangles, triangles, and squares are all examples of two-dimensional shapes. Incorporate geometric terms for two-dimensional shapes (shapes that have length and width, causing them to be flat) when describing items to your child. By putting names to the different shapes encountered in everyday life, identifying them will become second nature to your child, and this will aid in clarifying and understanding problems of geometry in later years.

Drawing Pictures Using Shapes. When your child is drawing a picture, point out the different shapes he is incorporating in the drawing. If he is drawing a picture of a person, you may point out that he has drawn a face in the shape of a circle and the arms in the shape of rectangles. If he is drawing a picture of a house, ask about the shape of the roof, the door, the windows, the chimney, and so on.

Abstract Pictures. Using construction paper, cut various examples of the four basic two-dimensional shapes (circle, rectangle, triangle, and square) in different sizes and colors. Have your child paste them on paper, making abstract pictures or designs. As your child works, talk to him about the shapes and how he is using them.

You can explain how two triangles can be joined to make a rectangle or how two small triangles can be joined to make one large triangle. You also can create some unique patterns with these shapes.

Geoboard Fun. Use a geoboard (a square board with pegs arranged in a 5 × 5 grid, available for a minimal cost at an educational store) and geobands (rubber bands) to explore the world of shapes. As your child uses the geoboard, challenge him with the following activities:

1. Ask him to make as many three-sided figures as he can. Explain that these are all called *triangles*. Many children have a single concept of a triangle in mind when they describe one. They need to understand that triangles can be different in size, shape, or position.

2. Ask him to make many different shapes that all have four equal sides. Explain that these are called *squares*. He will discover that squares can be small or large, but they are all the same shape.

3. Since all the pegs on the geoboard are labeled with the letters of the alphabet, ask him to use the geobands to make the rectangle with the corners *ADNK* and then make another rectangle with corners *GINL*. Later in his educational development, these points (corners) will be used to name rectangles.

The geoboard is a versatile manipulative that enables older children to discover advanced skills of creating formulas for area and perimeter, learn about sophisticated shapes, and become familiar with naming the coordinates of points on a plane. Children love this manipulative!

The Greedy Triangle. Read *The Greedy Triangle* by Marilyn Burns, and make the two-dimensional shapes mentioned in the book with a geoboard and geobands. This book describes many three-dimensional objects found in our world that are based on the two-dimensional shapes.

Three-Dimensional Shapes

Three-dimensional shapes include cubes, spheres, pyramids, cylinders, cones, and rectangular prisms. The important aspect of three-dimensional shapes is that they have depth or height in addition to length and width. After your child has learned the two-dimensional shapes, show him examples of the shapes listed above and have him use his knowledge about two-dimensional shapes to describe the three-dimensional shapes. Some examples may include:

A cube has six flat sides called *squares*.

A cylinder has two flat sides called *circles,* the bottom and the top.

A cone has one flat side called a *circle*.

Learn My Shape. This memory game will give your child practice learning the names of the three-dimensional shapes. Gather one object representative of each of the following solid shapes:

- Cone—ice cream cone, funnel, or a party hat
- Cylinder—vegetable can, soup can, paper towel roll, or a tube of lipstick
- Sphere—ball, globe, or an orange
- Rectangular prism (box)—cereal box, Jell-O box, shoebox, or book
- Cube—blocks, photograph cubes, or dice

Have your child identify each of the preceding shapes by their geometric names. A good way to do this is to place an example of each of the shapes on a table and have your child describe how they are different and how they are alike. Have him close his eyes while you remove one of the objects. See if he can determine and name which one of the geometric shapes is now missing.

Guess My Shape. Select one object for each three-dimensional shape from the preceding list. Place all the objects in a box, and have your child reach in the box and select one item. Without looking, have him describe to you the object in his hand while it is still in the box. He should be using terms such as *flat side, square,* or *circular,* which in essence is describing the object's two-dimensional shape, and depending on whether or not the selected object has a curved side (face), he should be articulating that as well. You try to guess the name of the shape he is holding. By reversing roles, you offer him an opportunity to visualize the objects through oral description.

My Shape Book. Make a book and have each page titled for one of the solid shapes listed above. Find pictures in magazines of items that represent these three-dimensional shapes, and paste them to the page that corresponds with the name of the shape.

Clay Shapes. Using Play-Doh or clay, make the six solid (i.e., three-dimensional) geometric shapes and label them. Using a butter knife will enable your child to make nice, neat sides with defined edges and corners.

Shape Walk. Take a walk in the neighborhood with your child, and record all the things you see that have a specific shape, and name the shape.

Symmetry

"Blob" Pictures. Fold a piece of construction paper in half, and then open it again and place a couple of dots of paint close to the fold. Have your child fold the paper and smooth out the paint. Open the paper, and a symmetrical shape (both sides match) is formed. Use only a little paint so that it does not extend off the paper when the paint is smoothed out. Point out that the fold is called the *line of symmetry,* meaning that when the shape is folded on this line, the two halves will be equal.

Fold and Cut. Fold a piece of construction paper in half. Cut any desired shape on the fold. Open the paper, and a symmetrical shape is formed. You can cut half an object such as a heart, snowman, or a paper doll so that when you open the paper, both sides are exactly the same (symmetrical).

Graphs

Graphs are "pictures" that compare collected information. All graphs should have a title explaining the information that is being shown. First grade children are introduced to the bar graph, presented in horizontal form (where the numbers are arranged horizontally, and the pictures of the objects are arranged vertically) and in vertical form (where the numbers are arranged vertically, and the pictures are arranged horizontally). Your child should be able to draw conclusions from a graph and make statements about the information that is being presented. He also should be able to collect, organize, and record data (information) by coloring in the appropriate number of squares on the graph and discussing the information depicted on the graph.

Make a Bar Graph. Using 1-inch graph paper, have your child select a topic of interest to graph. Suggestions include the color of the first 10 cars that go by his house, the number of the first 10 heads or tails that are tossed with a coin, the number of books he owns by four different authors, and even the eye colors of relatives in his family. Construct the bar graph for your child, including the information needed and the numbers from 1 to 10. Allow him to collect the data, title the bar graph, and record the information by coloring in the appropriate squares. Discuss the information that is presented. Have him practice making horizontal and vertical bar graphs.

Information that should be discussed includes the following: Most of my friends chose dogs as their favorite pet. Only one friend chose a fish as her favorite pet; two more friends chose dogs than they did cats, and the same number of friends chose fish as chose cats. The same information can be shown on a horizontal graph.

What Tests May Ask

Most standardized tests at this grade level don't ask very many obvious geometry questions. Instead, items involving geometry may appear as applied mathematics questions. There will be a few sections of the test that ask children to look at geometric shapes in a certain sequence and then complete or continue the pattern.

Other questions may ask a child to identify a shape by its name or to find an object (such as a pencil or soup can) with a comparable shape. For instance, a basketball is a sphere, and a can of soda is a cylinder.

Practice Skill: Geometry

Directions: Listen carefully to each question, and darken in the bubble beside the correct answer.

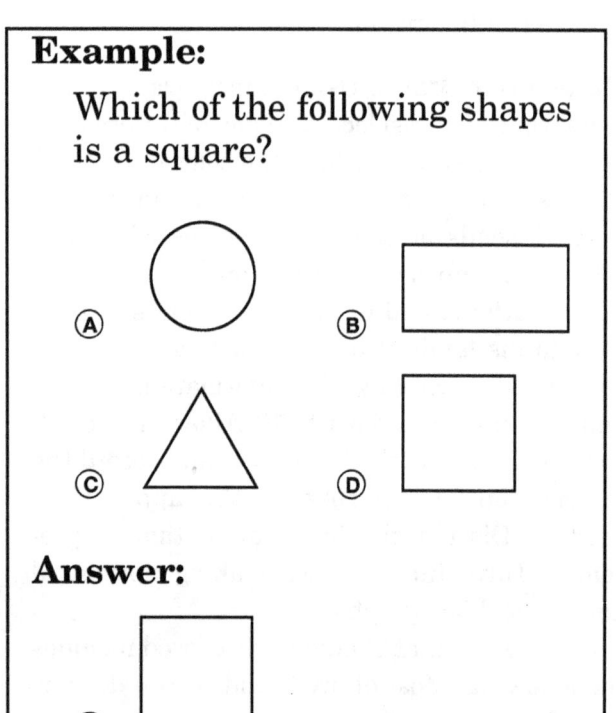

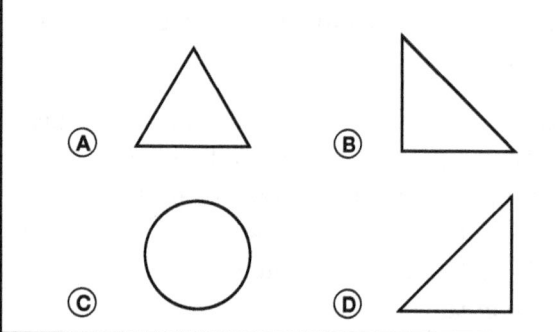

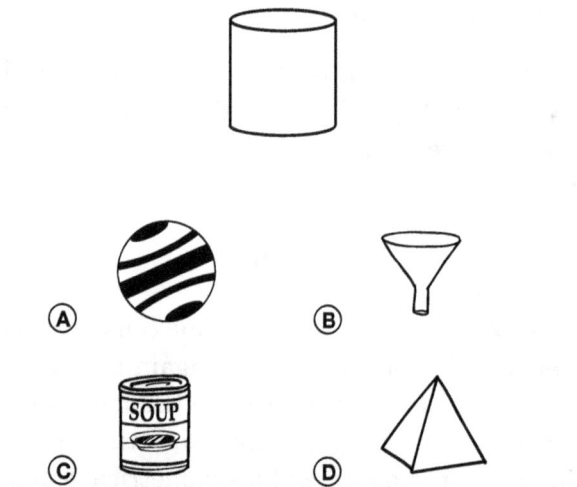

GEOMETRY

4 Which picture is a cone?

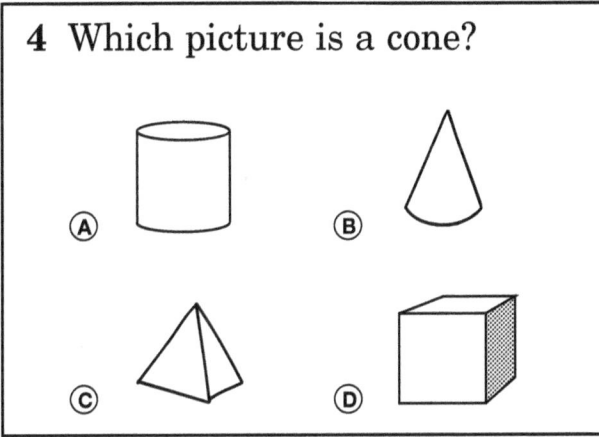

5 Which of the following shapes has sides that will match when it is folded on the dotted line?

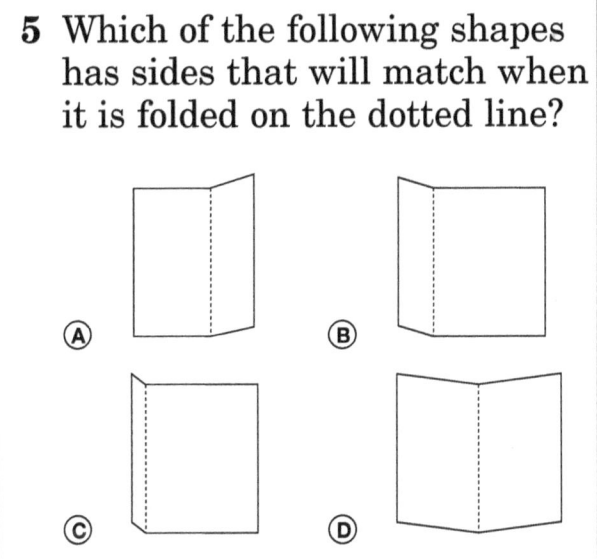

6 Which recess toy is enjoyed by the most children?

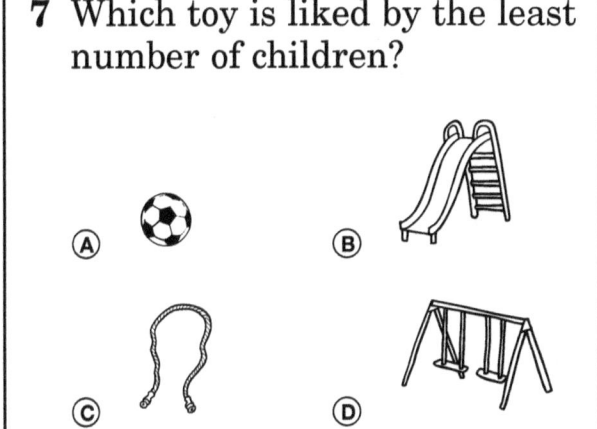

7 Which toy is liked by the least number of children?

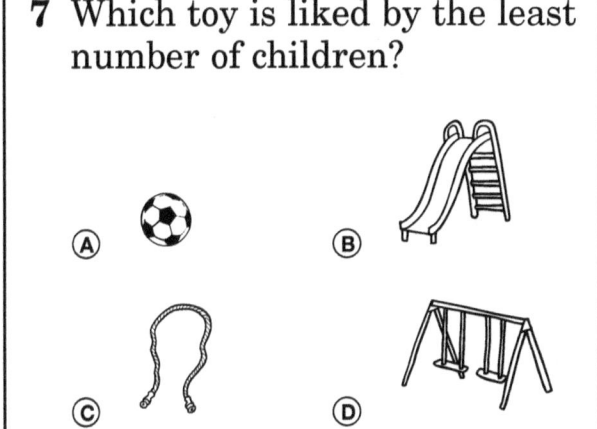

8 How many children liked playing ball the best?

Ⓐ 2
Ⓑ 3
Ⓒ 4
Ⓓ 5

Directions: Look at the graph below to answer questions 6 through 9.

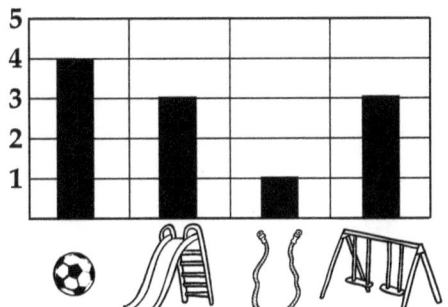

9 How many children in all liked playing on the swings and the slide?

Ⓐ 6

Ⓑ 3

Ⓒ 4

Ⓓ 5

(See pages 103–104 for answer key.)

CHAPTER 8

Fractions

These days, most schools follow the teaching of geometry with a unit on fractions. Sometimes they are combined into one area of study because in many ways they complement each other.

Geometry involves discussions about shapes, but the study of fractions teaches ways to break those same shapes into smaller equal pieces. Because learning about fractions combines many skills that children have been learning throughout first grade, they often study fractions near the end of the year. It is also a good way for children to build a foundation for their understanding of numbers less than one or parts of a whole.

Children often hear objects or shapes described in terms of fractions but are not always aware of the meaning of the terms. It's not uncommon for a child to ask, "May I have half?"

Many children use fraction terms in their language, but they are unable to describe what "half" is; also, they are often unfamiliar with how to write one-half ($\frac{1}{2}$).

What First Graders Should Know

When shown a picture of a shape that has dividing lines within the shape, first graders are expected to be able to decide if a shape is divided into equal parts. The fractions with a bottom number of 2, 3, and 4 are discussed and explored in first grade. Children should be able to name the fractional part of a shape that has a portion shaded, and they should be able to color in a fractional part of a shape.

First graders are also expected to be able to divide a group of objects into equal sets, and identify a fractional amount of the group. For instance, if there are 8 objects in a set and the child is asked, "How many objects are in $\frac{1}{4}$ of the set?" she should be able to divide the 8 objects into 4 equal groups, each group containing two objects. Since $\frac{1}{4}$ means 1 set out of 4 equal sets and one set contains 2 objects, then $\frac{1}{4}$ of 8 objects equals 2 objects.

What You and Your Child Can Do

Basics. Explain to your child that a *fraction* means a part of a whole; it is not the whole object or set. Demonstrate how to write the fraction *one-half* as $\frac{1}{2}$. Explain that the top number means "one part." The line dividing the numbers means "out of," and the bottom number means "2 equal parts," designating that the shape or set is divided into 2 equal parts.

Demonstrate writing the following fractions, and have your child read the fractions as explained above: $\frac{1}{3}$ (1 part out of 3 equal parts), $\frac{2}{3}$, $\frac{1}{4}$, $\frac{2}{4}$, $\frac{3}{4}$. Then practice reading the fractions as one-third, two-thirds, one-fourth or one-quarter, and so on.

Draw a square and divide it into two equal parts. Have your child color in $\frac{1}{2}$ of the shape. Continue by dividing shapes into 2, 3, and 4 equal parts and having your child color in $\frac{1}{4}$, $\frac{2}{4}$, $\frac{3}{4}$, $\frac{1}{3}$, and $\frac{2}{3}$.

MATH, GRADE ONE: GET READY!

Draw a set containing an equal number of objects, and divide them into 2 equal sets. Explain that one of the sets is equal to half of all the objects. For example, draw 8 stars. Divide them into 2 sets (each set has 4 stars). One-half means "1 set out of 2 sets," and since one set has 4 objects in it, "½ of 8 = 4." Try another problem: To find ⅔ of a group of 6 objects, divide the objects into 3 equal groups (the bottom number). Each set will have 2 objects in it. Since you want to find ⅔, you need to select 2 sets (each having 2 objects). Therefore, ⅔ of 6 objects = 4. (For first graders, the concept of fractions should not be complicated at this time with problems that involve numbers of objects that cannot be divided into equal sets, such as "Given 10 objects, find ⅓," or "How many cookies will Sally give away if she has 5 and gives away half?")

Fraction Food. Even a lunchtime sandwich can be used as an object lesson for teaching fractions. Have fun cutting a sandwich into halves and then quarters. Incorporate fraction terms in your discussion. Allow your child to eat ¾ of her sandwich before a cookie and ¼ after her cookie.

What Tests May Ask

You can expect a number of questions on a standardized test dealing with fractions in which students must identify a picture showing a given fraction or they will be asked to choose a fraction to match a picture. There will be one or two items that ask students to identify equal parts, and possibly a few showing fractions represented by objects in groups.

On many newer tests, children will find a written component that will ask for an answer as well as a sentence or two that explains the student's reasoning or thought processes. This is a skill that may require more practice than any other, so ask your child what made her choose an answer or complete a question in a certain way. Have her write it in a sentence and read it back to you.

Practice Skill: Fractions

Directions: Listen carefully to each question, and darken in the bubble beside the correct answer.

Example:

What fractional part of the shape below is shaded?

Ⓐ ½
Ⓑ ¼
Ⓒ ⅔
Ⓓ ⅛

Answer:

Ⓐ ½

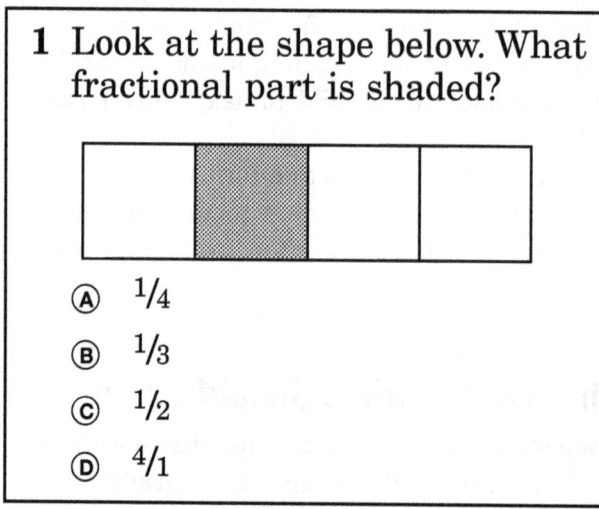

1 Look at the shape below. What fractional part is shaded?

Ⓐ ¼
Ⓑ ⅓
Ⓒ ½
Ⓓ 4/1

FRACTIONS

2 Which shape is divided into fourths?

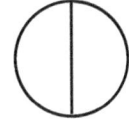

3 Which shape has ²/₃ shaded?

Ⓐ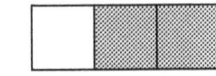

Ⓑ

Ⓒ

Ⓓ

4 Which drawing shows that 2 is ¹/₄ of 8?

Ⓐ

Ⓑ

Ⓒ

Ⓓ

5 How many apples would be one-fourth of this set?

Ⓐ 8 apples
Ⓑ 4 apples
Ⓒ 2 apples
Ⓓ 1 apple

6 How many pencils would be one-third of this set?

Ⓐ 1
Ⓑ 2
Ⓒ 3
Ⓓ 4

7 If you have 10 cookies and you give half of them away, how many do you give away?

Ⓐ 10
Ⓑ 2
Ⓒ 5
Ⓓ 8

59

8 If 14 people are invited to a party and only half of them can come, how many people can come?

- Ⓐ 14
- Ⓑ 2
- Ⓒ 7
- Ⓓ 5

(See page 104 for answer key.)

CHAPTER 9

Measurement

When we use measurement, we describe that which is being measured in terms of numbers, and those numbers then provide some concrete understanding or clarification in terms of length, temperature, weight, capacity, and so on. Measuring begins with selecting the appropriate measuring tool and making an estimate about the outcome. Once we complete the actual measuring, we can record the measurements and make comparisons about the findings.

What First Graders Should Know

Children in first grade begin their experiences with measuring by using nonstandard units of measurement. *Nonstandard units* used as measuring tools may include pencils, children's shoes, erasers, paper clips, and so on. Children discover the need for standard units of measurement (such as the inch, foot, cup, and pound) after experiencing situations in which many different answers are obtained when measuring the same object. In the classroom, for example, if children are asked to measure their math books using their individual pencils as the nonstandard unit of measurement, they will arrive at different answers because not all the pencils will be the same size. Different sized shoes, pencils, or glasses account for the variances in answers when measuring with nonstandard units of measurement.

Using nonstandard units of measurement allows children to grasp the concept of measuring. Children need to be actively involved with measuring. Children in first grade are encouraged to estimate a measurement after they have decided on an appropriate measuring tool. They learn how to measure and also how to use the appropriate terms of measurement. Length is measured in inches, feet, yards, and metric centimeters; capacity is measured using cups, pints, quarts, half-gallons, gallons, and metric liters; and weight is measured using pounds. After they are given information describing an equivalent relationship between two measurements (such as the fact that 2 cups = 1 pint), they are expected to be able to extend that relationship: If 2 cups = 1 pint, how many cups are in 3 pints?

First graders aren't expected to memorize equivalent relationships, but they should understand the approximate size of each standard measuring unit and know how to arrange those units from the smallest to the largest. First graders are also exposed to temperature measurement using a Fahrenheit thermometer. They should know an approximate thermometer reading for both winter and summer temperatures.

The unit of measurement for weight that is taught in first grade is the *pound*. A *balance scale* is usually used to compare the weight of an object in relation to a pound. A pound of margarine and a pound (pack) of clay are common items that can be used for one side of the balance to represent the pound. Different items can be placed on the other side of the scale to compare them to the pound and determine if they weigh more than or less than a pound. This will provide your child with a working conception of what constitutes the weight of a pound. Your child should have the opportunity to hold an object that weighs a pound in order to get a feel for its weight.

What You and Your Child Can Do

Nonstandard Measures. Allow your child to learn to measure length using a pencil as his measuring tool. Measure the lengths of different items in the house such as the television, a game box, a bookshelf, or a shoe while you measure the same items using a different sized pencil. Record the information, and discuss the discrepancies. Allow your child to measure capacity using a small teacup of water as a measuring tool while you use a large coffee mug. Measure the capacity of several different sized glasses, pitchers, or bowls in the house. Record the results, and discuss the discrepancies. Help your child discover that familiar measuring units such as pints, quarts, or half-gallons are needed so that measurements are meaningful to everyone.

How Big Is a Foot? With your child, read *How Big Is a Foot?* by Rolf Myller, which illustrates the importance of standard units of measurement.

Measuring Length and Capacity

Ruler Rules. Teach your child how to align a ruler with an object to be measured. A common mistake many children make is to align the object with the number 1 on the ruler as opposed to aligning it with the beginning of the ruler. After the object is aligned, explain that the measurement of the object will be the number on the tool that is closest to where the object ends. Explain the calibrations as well as the terms *inch, foot,* and *yard.* Allow your child to estimate and measure items around the house with the ruler. Emphasize that estimates are nonexact answers, but nonetheless, estimating is an important skill to learn. After your child has practiced measuring many items, his estimation skills should improve. Estimation involves making judgments and having a frame of reference. Practice with estimation, verification (measuring), and comparison are the best way to improve estimating skills.

Measure Me. Using a piece of string, measure your child's foot, marking the string to indicate the measurement, and then align the string along the numbers of a ruler. This exercise will allow your child to see an object (his foot) expressed comparatively in terms of inches. Continue this exercise by measuring your child's arm, his leg, his little finger, the circumference of his head, the distance between his knee and foot, the distance between his forehead and the tip of his nose, and his height. Don't forget to record your results; this is important because it allows your child to compare measurements.

Inch by Inch. Here's another good book: Leo Lionni's *Inch by Inch.* Read this with your child, and measure—as the inchworm does—all the parts of the animals in the story.

Measurement Search. Make three columns on a piece of paper and label them *inch, foot,* and *yard.* Look through the house and find as many things as you can that are about the size of an inch, a foot, and a yard. Which measurement unit was the easiest to find?

All the Way Around. Measure the perimeter (distance around) of objects, such as a book, a table, a toy chest, or a shoebox. Make shapes on a geoboard (mentioned in Chapter 7), and measure the perimeters.

Measuring Capacity. Allow your child to experiment with measuring capacity by using water and several different sized containers. Let him explore the relationships between tall, thin containers and short, wide containers. Pour water from one container into another, and make comparisons. Practice using the standard cup, pint, quart, half-gallon, and gallon by pouring the water again from one container into the other for the purpose of making equivalencies (equal amounts). Allow your child to keep a log, recording any equivalencies that are discovered. After the relationships are made, set up several problems for your child to explore. How many cups are in 4 pints? How many pints are in 2 quarts? Lead him to discover and generalize that if 2 pints are in 1 quart, then 4 pints are in 2 quarts, and 6 pints are in 3 quarts. After he has actually done the experiments, he should be able to visualize or formulate a mental picture of the relationship that two small containers can fill one larger container and that this process repeats itself. The experimentation stage, or *concrete stage,* is vital for understanding the measurement concepts so that your child can do the abstract problems with a mental image of the process. Use an empty 2-liter soda bottle, and experiment to find out about how much liquid 1 liter would contain. Ask your child to determine about how many cups would be in a 1-liter container. If the use of water presents a problem, rice makes a fine substitute for measuring capacity.

I'm the Chef. Allow your child to help with measuring when you are cooking and following a recipe. Allow him to pour his own cereal using a measuring cup. Discover if he normally eats more than a cup or less than a cup of cereal. Is it a different amount for different kinds of cereals?

Measuring Mass (Weight)

How Heavy Are You? Using the balance scale and an object weighing a pound, place the object on one side of the scale. Find other objects in the house that weigh about a pound, and predict if they are lighter or heavier than the pound. Verify your answers by placing the items on the scale, and record the results.

Shopping Trip. Allow your child to go to the grocery store with you and use the scales in the store to weigh produce. Have him try to estimate a pound of an item, and then weigh it for accuracy. Try several different items, making your child aware that the number of items in a pound will vary, depending on the item. Point out that many grocery items are priced by the pound.

Measuring Temperature. Explain to your child that mercury is the silver substance in the thermometer and that it responds to the temperature in the air (stress to your child that mercury is a highly toxic substance and should never be handled outside the thermometer's protective glass enclosure). If the air is hot, the mercury expands; if the air is cold, the mercury contracts. Teach him how to read the thermometer calibrations. The smaller lines between the bold lines with numbers represent a certain number of degrees.

Weather Watch. Purchase an inexpensive thermometer, and place it in an accessible location outdoors so that your child can check and record the temperature on a daily basis.

What Tests May Ask

Most of the measurement questions asked on standardized tests probably will show a picture of a measurement tool and ask the child to read what a certain object measures. For example, it might show a thermometer and ask, "What is the temperature shown?" Or it might show a ruler next to a stick and ask, "How long is this stick?"

Tests also usually will ask students to measure the perimeter of a shape or to determine the perimeter of a rectangle given the length of two of the sides. Other measurement questions may be in the form of a word or story problem. In addition, measurement concepts may be combined with other math skills in two- or three-step problems.

Practice Skill: Measuring

Directions: Listen carefully to each question, and darken in the bubble beside the correct answer.

Example:

What tool should be used to measure milk?

- Ⓐ a ruler
- Ⓑ a thermometer
- Ⓒ a measuring cup
- Ⓓ a scale

Answer:

Ⓒ a measuring cup

1. What tool should be used to measure apples?
   - Ⓐ a scale
   - Ⓑ a ruler
   - Ⓒ a measuring cup
   - Ⓓ a thermometer

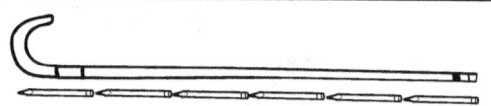

2. Look at the picture above. How many pencils long is the cane?
   - Ⓐ 2
   - Ⓑ 4
   - Ⓒ 6
   - Ⓓ 7

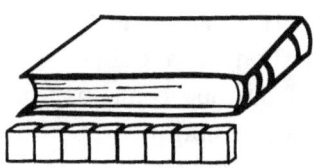

3. Look at the picture above. How many blocks long is the book?
   - Ⓐ 5
   - Ⓑ 6
   - Ⓒ 8
   - Ⓓ 9

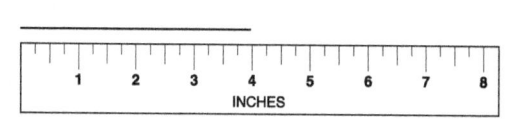

4. Look at the picture above. How long is the line?
   - Ⓐ 3 inches
   - Ⓑ 4 inches
   - Ⓒ 6 inches
   - Ⓓ 4 centimeters

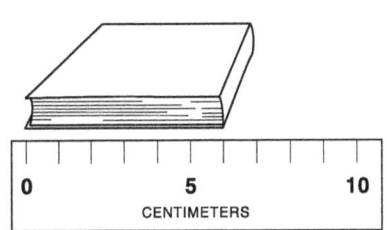

5 Look at the picture above. How long is the book?
- Ⓐ 6 inches
- Ⓑ 5 centimeters
- Ⓒ 6 centimeters
- Ⓓ 10 centimeters

6 If 2 cups equal 1 pint, how many cups are in 2 pints?
- Ⓐ 2
- Ⓑ 1
- Ⓒ 3
- Ⓓ 4

7 If 2 quarts equal one-half gallon, how many half-gallons would 6 quarts make?
- Ⓐ 2
- Ⓑ 3
- Ⓒ 6
- Ⓓ 8

8 Look at the picture above. The butter in the picture weighs 1 pound. How much does the book weigh?
- Ⓐ It weighs more than 1 pound.
- Ⓑ It weights less than 1 pound.
- Ⓒ It weights 5 pounds.
- Ⓓ It weighs 1 pound.

9 The clay in the picture above weighs 1 pound. What does the scale show you about the doll?
- Ⓐ It weighs more than 1 pound.
- Ⓑ It weighs less than 1 pound.
- Ⓒ It weighs 5 pounds.
- Ⓓ It weighs 1 pound.

10 Look at the picture above. What would the thermometer read on this kind of day?

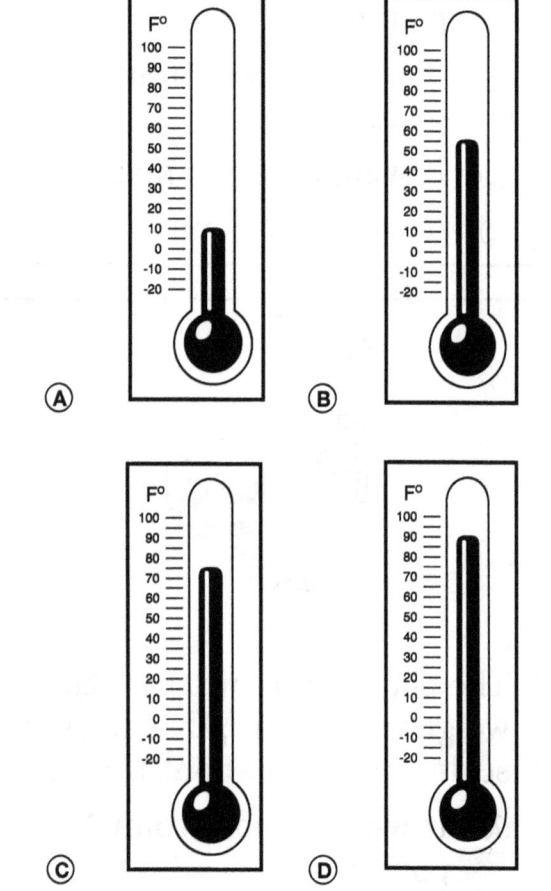

11 Look at the picture above. What would the thermometer read on this kind of day?

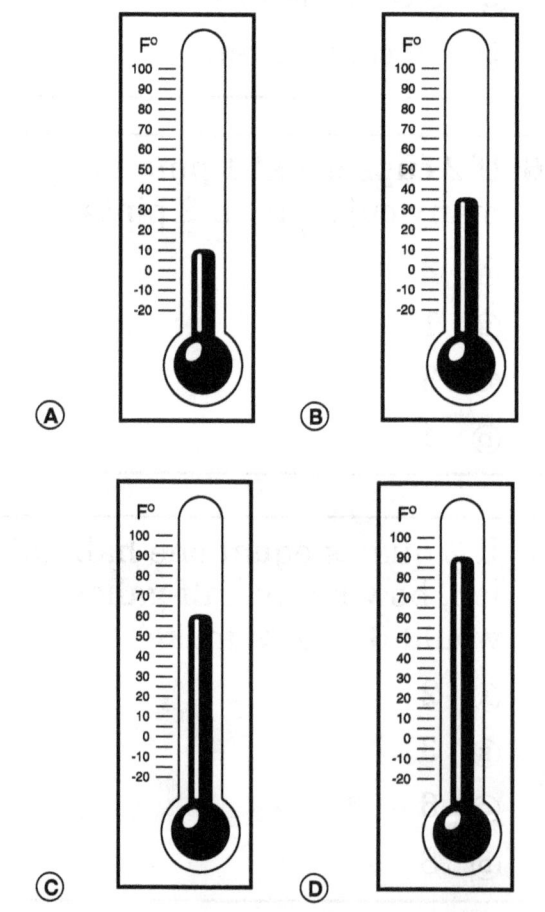

12 Look at each picture below. Which item holds more than 1 liter?

(See page 104 for answer key.)

CHAPTER 10

Solving Word Problems

Word problems sometimes present unique challenges for first graders because the children are required to perform multiple tasks to arrive at an answer to a given question. Word problems involve processing ideas conveyed by both words and numbers for the purpose of determining a relationship between them and, finally, a solution. A parent's explanations and demonstrations as to how to solve word problems are important, but children need to be actively involved in their learning by manipulating objects, experimenting, and actually trying out their own strategies.

Solving word problems presents an opportunity for children to explore how and when to use numbers and to begin to organize information and think logically. Real-life experiences with numbers and solving word problems allow children to make sense of the math concepts that are taught and to understand why math is learned. For instance, when a child is learning addition (or subtraction, fractions, and so on), it's important to bring meaning to the process by incorporating a story problem relevant to addition: Mary has three flowers, and she gets two more. How many does she have now? This story problem attaches meaning to the process of adding 3 + 2. Solving number problems is a useful skill because it promotes higher forms of learning and thinking. With word problems, children need to apply their knowledge about numbers and employ reasoning skills.

What First Graders Should Know

Word problems in first grade concentrate primarily on joining two sets (adding), separating a number of objects from a set (subtracting), and comparing two sets of objects (subtracting). Translating the word problem into a visual representation is done with the use of *manipulatives* such as beans, marshmallows, or poker chips (the choice is limited to your imagination). These manipulatives, which represent the objects in a word problem, enable your child to "act out" the problem. This brings meaning to the abstract.

After your child has had many experiences using manipulatives, she should be able to translate the problem into a drawing involving simple markings, such as circles or dots, which in essence replace the manipulatives, and write a number sentence to match. For example, let's look at this problem: Joe has three cookies, and his friend gives him one more. How many does he have now? Your child should translate the word problem on paper in the following form:

$$ooo \quad o \quad (3 + 1 = 4)$$

Finally, she should advance to the abstract stage so that she is able to form a mental image of the story problem and write the number sentence.

What You and Your Child Can Do

"Think Alouds." After reading a word problem, demonstrate for your child how to solve the problem using the following steps:

- Restate the problem using your own words.
- Discuss an appropriate method to organize the given information.
- Decide what information is necessary to solve the problem.
- Choose the number operation (addition or subtraction) that is appropriate.
- Use concrete objects to represent the items in the problem.
- Write the number sentence to match the story problem.
- Solve the number sentence.
- Decide if the solution is reasonable.

Encourage your child to perform "think alouds" as she solves word problems. This provides her with an opportunity to articulate her thought processes, stay focused, and receive support from you as needed.

I Change It To... Solve word problems with your child by encouraging her to follow the steps listed above. After the solution is found, alter an aspect of the problem so that it forms a new problem to be solved. For example, Neil is 3 years older than Jane, who is 12 years old. How old is Neil? Neil is 3 years *younger* than Jane, who is 12 years old. How old is Neil? Ask leading questions where applicable. This creates an atmosphere for critical thinking and prepares your child to learn how to develop her own new problems.

Creating original word problems is a more difficult skill and requires your child to provide the information needed to solve a problem. A beginning stage may be to provide the information for your child and allow her to discover how the information can be used to formulate a new word problem.

What Tests May Ask

Standardized tests for first grade will present a number of word problems for each type of math skill. Rather than having one section of word problems, your child probably will encounter word problems in addition and subtraction sections of the test. The test will present the word problems and then offer your child a range of possible answers.

Practice Skill: Solving Word Problems

Directions: Listen carefully to each question, and darken in the bubble beside the correct answer.

Example:

Joe has 3 red balloons and 5 yellow balloons. How many balloons does he have in all?

- Ⓐ 2
- Ⓑ 8
- Ⓒ 6
- Ⓓ 7

Answer:

- Ⓑ 8

---

1 Art has 5 baseballs, and he loses 2. How many does he have left?

- Ⓐ 4
- Ⓑ 3
- Ⓒ 2
- Ⓓ 7

SOLVING WORD PROBLEMS

2 Seven children are playing on the swings. Three more children join them on the swings. How many children are on the swings now?
- (A) 10
- (B) 4
- (C) 9
- (D) 11

3 There are 8 horses in the barn, and 2 run out to the field. How many are left in the barn?
- (A) 10
- (B) 6
- (C) 7
- (D) 5

4 There are 9 oranges and 4 apples on the table. How many more oranges than apples are on the table?
- (A) 13
- (B) 5
- (C) 6
- (D) 4

5 There are 7 girls and 9 boys invited to the party. How many fewer girls are invited to the party?
- (A) 16
- (B) 3
- (C) 2
- (D) 6

6 Mary buys a pencil for 2 cents, a book for 5 cents, and an eraser for 4 cents. How much do these items cost in all?
- (A) 7 cents
- (B) 9 cents
- (C) 6 cents
- (D) 11 cents

7 Pat has 2 quarters and a dime. He spends 30 cents. How much does he have left?
- (A) 60 cents
- (B) 32 cents
- (C) 28 cents
- (D) 30 cents

8 Carol has 6 inches of ribbon. She wants to cut the ribbon into pieces that are 3 inches long. How many pieces can she make?

- Ⓐ 6
- Ⓑ 9
- Ⓒ 3
- Ⓓ 2

9 How many wheels are on 3 cars if each car has 4 wheels?

- Ⓐ 7
- Ⓑ 1
- Ⓒ 12
- Ⓓ 9

10 Mom baked 10 cookies for the party. Five children are coming to the party. If each child gets the same number of cookies, how many cookies will each child get?

- Ⓐ 15
- Ⓑ 10
- Ⓒ 2
- Ⓓ 5

11 A doll costs 5 cents. A bat costs 7 cents. A pack of crayons costs 3 cents. How much will a doll and 2 packs of crayons cost?

- Ⓐ 15 cents
- Ⓑ 12 cents
- Ⓒ 11 cents
- Ⓓ 13 cents

12 There are 7 worms, and a bird eats 1 of them. How many worms are left?

- Ⓐ 8
- Ⓑ 1
- Ⓒ 7
- Ⓓ 6

13 There are 6 balloons for 2 children. How many balloons does each child receive if each child gets the same number of balloons?

- Ⓐ 6
- Ⓑ 4
- Ⓒ 3
- Ⓓ 8

SOLVING WORD PROBLEMS

14 There are 8 bees and 3 flowers. How many more bees are there than flowers?
- Ⓐ 8
- Ⓑ 5
- Ⓒ 11
- Ⓓ 38

15 There were 12 toys in the store, and 8 were bought. How many toys are left in the store?
- Ⓐ 20
- Ⓑ 12
- Ⓒ 5
- Ⓓ 4

(See page 104 for answer key.)

APPENDIX A

Web Sites and Resources for More Information

Homework

Homework Central
http://www.HomeworkCentral.com
Terrific site for students, parents, and teachers, filled with information, projects, and more.

Win the Homework Wars
(Sylvan Learning Centers)
http://www.educate.com/online/qa_peters.html

Reading and Grammar Help

Born to Read: How to Raise a Reader
http://www.ala.org/alsc/raise_a_reader.html

Guide to Grammar and Writing
http://webster.commnet.edu/hp/pages/darling/grammar.htm
Help with "plague words and phrases," grammar FAQs, sentence parts, punctuation, rules for common usage.

Internet Public Library: Reading Zone
http://www.ipl.org/cgi-bin/youth/youth.out

Keeping Kids Reading and Writing
http://www.tiac.net/users/maryl/

U.S. Dept. of Education: Helping Your Child Learn to Read
http://www.ed.gov/pubs/parents/Reading/index.html

Math Help

Center for Advancement of Learning
http://www.muskingum.edu/%7Ecal/database/Math2.html
Substitution and memory strategies for math.

Center for Advancement of Learning
http://www.muskingum.edu/%7Ecal/database/Math1.html
General tips and suggestions.

Math.com
http://www.math.com
The world of math online.

Math.com
http://www.math.com/student/testprep.html
Get ready for standardized tests.

Math.com: Homework Help in Math
http://www.math.com/students/homework.html

Math.com: Math for Homeschoolers
http://www.math.com/parents/homeschool.html

The Math Forum: Problems and Puzzles
http://forum.swarthmore.edu/library/resource_types/problems_puzzles
Lots of fun math puzzles and problems for grades K through 12.

The Math Forum: Math Tips and Tricks
http://forum.swarthmore.edu/k12/mathtips/mathtips.html

Tips on Testing

Books on Test Preparation
http://www.testbooksonline.com/preHS.asp
This site provides printed resources for parents who wish to help their children prepare for standardized school tests.

Core Knowledge Web Site
http://www.coreknowledge.org/
Site dedicated to providing resources for parents; based on the books of E. D. Hirsch, Jr., who wrote the *What Your X Grader Needs to Know* series.

Family Education Network
http://www.familyeducation.com/article/0,1120,1-6219,00.html
This report presents some of the arguments against current standardized testing practices in the public schools. The site also provides links to family activities that help kids learn.

Math.com
http://www.math.com/students/testprep.html
Get ready for standardized tests.

Standardized Tests
http://arc.missouri.edu/k12/
K through 12 assessment tools and know-how.

Parents: Testing in Schools

KidSource: Talking to Your Child's Teacher about Standardized Tests
http://www.kidsource.com/kidsource/content2/talking.assessment.k12.4.html
This site provides basic information to help parents understand their children's test results and provides pointers for how to discuss the results with their children's teachers.

eSCORE.com: State Test and Education Standards
http://www.eSCORE.com
Find out if your child meets the necessary requirements for your local schools. A Web site with experts from Brazelton Institute and Harvard's Project Zero.

Overview of States' Assessment Programs
http://ericae.net/faqs/

Parent Soup
Education Central: Standardized Tests
http://www.parentsoup.com/edcentral/testing
A parent's guide to standardized testing in the schools, written from a parent advocacy standpoint.

National Center for Fair and Open Testing, Inc. (FairTest)
342 Broadway
Cambridge, MA 02139
(617) 864-4810
http://www.fairtest.org

National Parent Information Network
http://npin.org

Publications for Parents from the U.S. Department of Education
http://www.ed.gov/pubs/parents/
An ever-changing list of information for parents available from the U.S. Department of Education.

State of the States Report
http://www.edweek.org/sreports/qc99/states/indicators/in-intro.htm
A report on testing and achievement in the 50 states.

Testing: General Information

Academic Center for Excellence
http://www.acekids.com

American Association for Higher Education Assessment
http://www.aahe.org/assessment/web.htm

American Educational Research Association (AERA)
http://aera.net
An excellent link to reports on American education, including reports on the controversy over standardized testing.

American Federation of Teachers
555 New Jersey Avenue, NW
Washington, D.C. 20011

APPENDIX A

Association of Test Publishers Member Products and Services
http://www.testpublishers.org/memserv.htm

Education Week on the Web
http://www.edweek.org

ERIC Clearinghouse on Assessment and Evaluation
1131 Shriver Lab
University of Maryland
College Park, MD 20742
http://ericae.net
A clearinghouse of information on assessment and education reform.

FairTest: The National Center for Fair and Open Testing
http://fairtest.org/facts/ntfact.htm
http://fairtest.org/
The National Center for Fair and Open Testing is an advocacy organization working to end the abuses, misuses, and flaws of standardized testing and to ensure that evaluation of students and workers is fair, open, and educationally sound. This site provides many links to fact sheets, opinion papers, and other sources of information about testing.

National Congress of Parents and Teachers
700 North Rush Street
Chicago, Illinois 60611

National Education Association
1201 16th Street, NW
Washington, DC 20036

National School Boards Association
http://www.nsba.org
A good source for information on all aspects of public education, including standardized testing.

Testing Our Children: A Report Card on State Assessment Systems
http://www.fairtest.org/states/survey.htm
Report of testing practices of the states, with graphical links to the states and a critique of fair testing practices in each state.

Trends in Statewide Student Assessment Programs: A Graphical Summary
http://www.ccsso.org/survey96.html
Results of annual survey of states' departments of public instruction regarding their testing practices.

U.S. Department of Education
http://www.ed.gov/

Web Links for Parents Who Want to Help Their Children Achieve
http://www.liveandlearn.com/learn.html
This page offers many Web links to free and for-sale information and materials for parents who want to help their children do well in school. Titles include such free offerings as the Online Colors Game and questionnaires to determine whether your child is ready for school.

What Should Parents Know about Standardized Testing in the Schools?
http://www.rusd.k12.ca.us/parents/standard.html
An online brochure about standardized testing in the schools, with advice regarding how to become an effective advocate for your child.

Test Publishers Online

ACT: Information for Life's Transitions
http://www.act.org

American Guidance Service, Inc.
http://www.agsnet.com

Ballard & Tighe Publishers
http://www.ballard-tighe.com

Consulting Psychologists Press
http://www.cpp-db.com

CTB McGraw-Hill
http://www.ctb.com

Educational Records Bureau
http://www.erbtest.org/index.html

Educational Testing Service
http://www.ets.org

General Educational Development (GED) Testing Service
http://www.acenet.edu/calec/ged/home.html

Harcourt Brace Educational Measurement
http://www.hbem.com

Piney Mountain Press—A Cyber-Center for Career and Applied Learning
http://www.pineymountain.com

ProEd Publishing
http://www.proedinc.com

Riverside Publishing Company
http://www.hmco.com/hmco/riverside

Stoelting Co.
http://www.stoeltingco.com

Sylvan Learning Systems, Inc.
http://www.educate.com

Touchstone Applied Science Associates, Inc. (TASA)
http://www.tasa.com

Tests Online

(*Note:* We don't endorse tests; some may not have technical documentation. Evaluate the quality of any testing program before making decisions based on its use.)

Edutest, Inc.
http://www.edutest.com
Edutest is an Internet-accessible testing service that offers criterion-referenced tests for elementary school students, based upon the standards for K through 12 learning and achievement in the states of Virginia, California, and Florida.

Virtual Knowledge
http://www.smarterkids.com
This commercial service, which enjoys a formal partnership with Sylvan Learning Centers, offers a line of skills assessments for preschool through grade 9 for use in the classroom or the home. For free online sample tests, see the Virtual Test Center.

APPENDIX B

Read More about It

Abbamont, Gary W. *Test Smart: Ready-to-Use Test-Taking Strategies and Activities for Grades 5–12*. Upper Saddle River, NJ: Prentice Hall Direct, 1997.

Cookson, Peter W., and Joshua Halberstam. *A Parent's Guide to Standardized Tests in School: How to Improve Your Child's Chances for Success*. New York: Learning Express, 1998.

Frank, Steven, and Stephen Frank. *Test-Taking Secrets: Study Better, Test Smarter, and Get Great Grades (The Backpack Study Series)*. Holbrook, MA: Adams Media Corporation, 1998.

Gilbert, Sara Dulaney. *How to Do Your Best on Tests: A Survival Guide*. New York: Beech Tree Books, 1998.

Gruber, Gary. *Dr. Gary Gruber's Essential Guide to Test-Taking for Kids, Grades 3–5*. New York: William Morrow & Co., 1986.

———. *Gary Gruber's Essential Guide to Test-Taking for Kids, Grades 6, 7, 8, 9*. New York: William Morrow & Co., 1997.

Leonhardt, Mary. *99 Ways to Get Kids to Love Reading and 100 Books They'll Love*. New York: Crown, 1997.

———. *Parents Who Love Reading, Kids Who Don't: How It Happens and What You Can Do about It*. New York: Crown, 1995.

McGrath, Barbara B. *The Baseball Counting Book*. Watertown, MA: Charlesbridge, 1999.

———. *More M&M's Brand Chocolate Candies Math*. Watertown, MA: Charlesbridge, 1998.

Mokros, Janice R. *Beyond Facts & Flashcards: Exploring Math with Your Kids*. Portsmouth, NH: Heinemann, 1996.

Romain, Trevor, and Elizabeth Verdick. *True or False?: Tests Stink!* Minneapolis: Free Spirit Publishing Co., 1999.

Schartz, Eugene M. *How to Double Your Child's Grades in School: Build Brilliance and Leadership into Your Child—from Kindergarten to College—in Just 5 Minutes a Day*. New York: Barnes & Noble, 1999.

Taylor, Kathe, and Sherry Walton. *Children at the Center: A Workshop Approach to Standardized Test Preparation, K–8*. Portsmouth, NH: Heinemann, 1998.

Tobia, Sheila. *Overcoming Math Anxiety*. New York: W. W. Norton & Company, Inc., 1995.

Tufariello, Ann Hunt. *Up Your Grades: Proven Strategies for Academic Success*. Lincolnwood, IL: VGM Career Horizons, 1996.

Vorderman, Carol. *How Math Works*. Pleasantville, NY: Reader's Digest Association, Inc., 1996.

Zahler, Kathy A. *50 Simple Things You Can Do to Raise a Child Who Loves to Read*. New York: IDG Books, 1997.

APPENDIX C

What Your Child's Test Scores Mean

Several weeks or months after your child has taken standardized tests, you will receive a report such as the TerraNova Home Report found in Figures 1 and 2. You will receive similar reports if your child has taken other tests. We briefly examine what information the reports include.

Look at the first page of the Home Report. Note that the chart provides labeled bars showing the child's performance. Each bar is labeled with the child's National Percentile for that skill area. When you know how to interpret them, national percentiles can be the most useful scores you encounter on reports such as this. Even when you are confronted with different tests that use different scale scores, you can always interpret percentiles the same way, regardless of the test. A percentile tells the percent of students who score at or below that level. A percentile of 25, for example, means that 25 percent of children taking the test scored at or below that score. (It also means that 75 percent of students scored above that score.) Note that the average is always at the 50th percentile.

On the right side of the graph on the first page of the report, the publisher has designated the ranges of scores that constitute average, above average, and below average. You can also use this slightly more precise key for interpreting percentiles:

PERCENTILE RANGE	LEVEL
2 and Below	Deficient
3–8	Borderline
9–23	Low Average
24–75	Average
76–97	High Average
98 and Up	Superior

The second page of the Home report provides a listing of the child's strengths and weaknesses, along with keys for mastery, partial mastery, and non-mastery of the skills. Scoring services determine these breakdowns based on the child's scores as compared with those from the national norm group.

Your child's teacher or guidance counselor will probably also receive a profile report similar to the TerraNova Individual Profile Report, shown in Figures 3 and 4. That report will be kept in your child's permanent record. The first aspect of this report to notice is that the scores are expressed both numerically and graphically.

First look at the score bands under National Percentile. Note that the scores are expressed as bands, with the actual score represented by a dot within each band. The reason we express the scores as bands is to provide an idea of the amount by which typical scores may vary for each student. That is, each band represents a

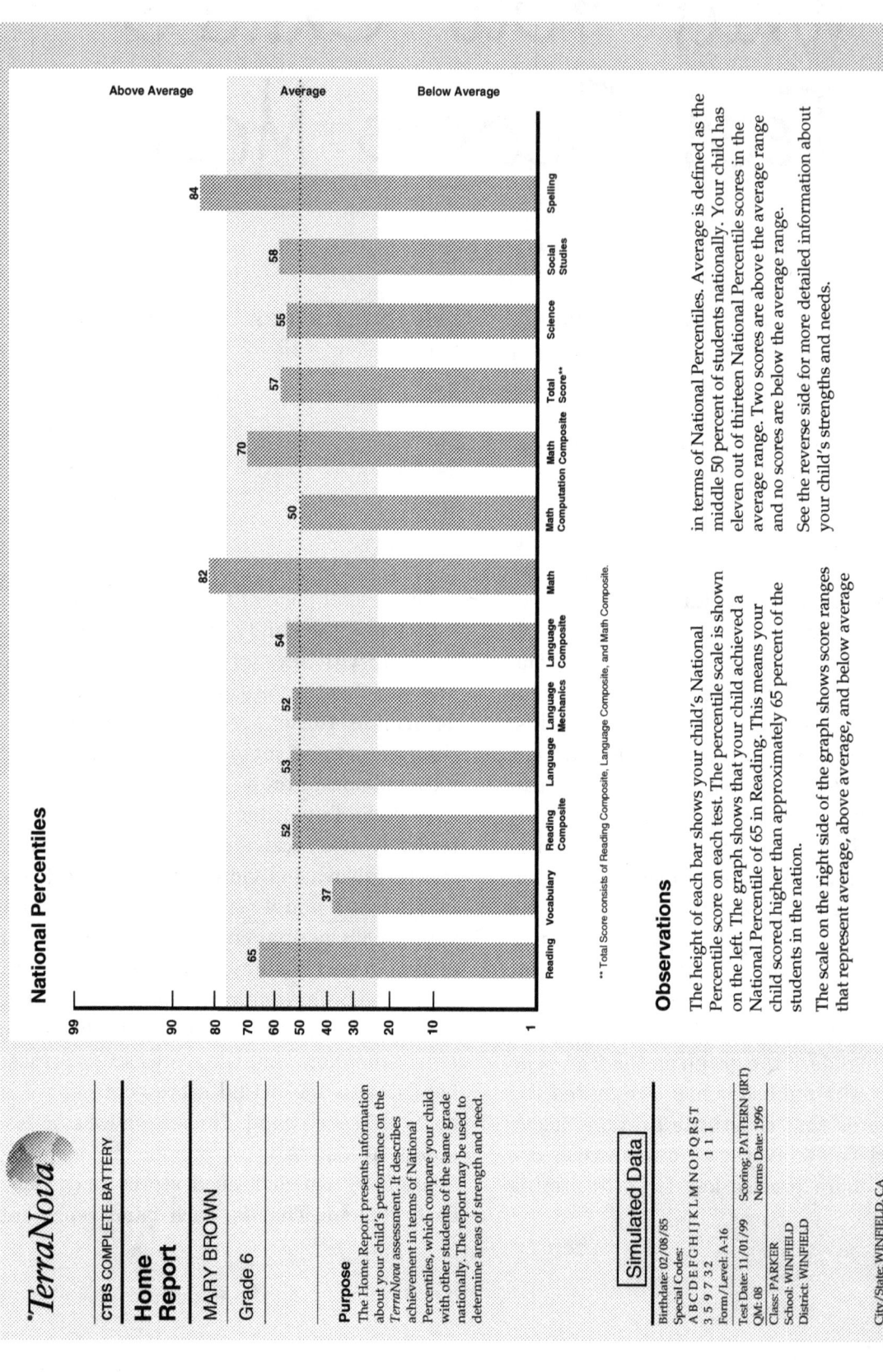

Figure 1 (SOURCE: CTB/McGraw-Hill, copyright © 1997. All rights reserved. Reproduced with permission.)

APPENDIX C

TerraNova

CTBS COMPLETE BATTERY

Home Report

MARY BROWN

Grade 6

Purpose

This page of the Home Report presents information about your child's strengths and needs. This information is provided to help you monitor your child's academic growth.

Simulated Data

Birthdate: 02/08/85
Special Codes:
A B C D E F G H I J K L M N O P Q R S T
3 5 9 7 3 2   1 1 1
Form/Level: A-16   Scoring: PATTERN (IRT)
Test Date: 11/01/99 Norms Date: 1996
QM: 08
Class: PARKER
School: WINFIELD
District: WINFIELD

City/State: WINFIELD, CA

CTB McGraw-Hill

Page 2

Strengths

Reading
● Basic Understanding
● Analyze Text

Vocabulary
● Word Meaning
● Words in Context

Language
● Editing Skills
● Sentence Structure

Language Mechanics
● Sentences, Phrases, Clauses

Mathematics
● Computation and Numerical Estimation
● Operation Concepts

Mathematics Computation
● Add Whole Numbers
● Multiply Whole Numbers

Science
● Life Science
● Inquiry Skills

Social Studies
● Geographic Perspectives
● Economic Perspectives

Spelling
● Vowels
● Consonants

Key ● Mastery

Needs

Reading
● Evaluate and Extend Meaning
○ Identify Reading Strategies

Vocabulary
○ Multimeaning Words

Language
● Writing Strategies

Language Mechanics
○ Writing Conventions

Mathematics
● Measurement
● Geometry and Spatial Sense

Mathematics Computation
○ Percents

Science
○ Earth and Space Science

Social Studies
● Historical and Cultural Perspectives

Spelling
No area of needs were identified for this content area

Key ○ Partial Mastery   ○ Non-Mastery

General Interpretation

The left column shows your child's best areas of performance. In each case, your child has reached mastery level. The column at the right shows the areas within each test section where your child's scores are the lowest. In these cases, your child has not reached mastery level, although he or she may have reached partial mastery.

Copyright © 1997 CTB/McGraw-Hill. All rights reserved.

Figure 2 (SOURCE: CTB/McGraw-Hill, copyright © 1997. All rights reserved. Reproduced with permission.)

MATH, GRADE ONE: GET READY!

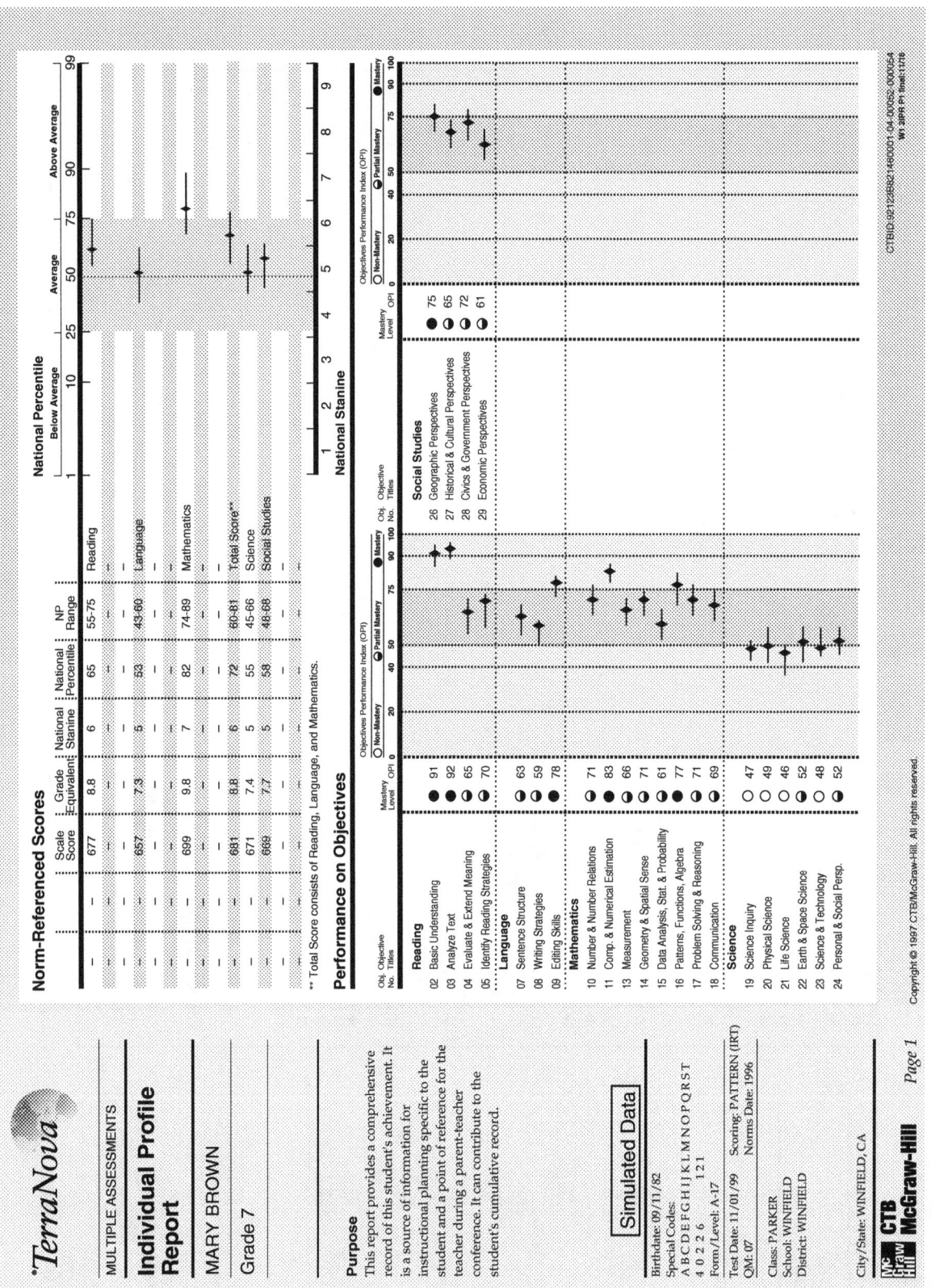

Figure 3 (SOURCE: CTB/McGraw-Hill, copyright © 1997. All rights reserved. Reproduced with permission.)

APPENDIX C

Figure 4 (SOURCE: CTB/McGraw-Hill, copyright © 1997. All rights reserved. Reproduced with permission.)

MATH, GRADE ONE: GET READY!

TerraNova

MULTIPLE ASSESSMENTS

Student Performance Level Report

KEN ALLEN

Grade 4

Purpose

This report describes this student's achievement in terms of five performance levels for each content area. The meaning of these levels is described on the back of this page. Performance levels are a new way of describing achievement.

Simulated Data

Birthdate: 02/08/86
Special Codes:
A B C D E F G H I J K L M N O P Q R S T
3 5 9 7 3 2   1 1 1
Form/Level: A-14
Test Date: 04/15/97   Scoring: PATTERN (IRT)
QM: 31   Norms Date: 1996
Class: SCHWARZ
School: WINFIELD
District: GREEN VALLEY

City/State: WINFIELD, CA

CTB McGraw-Hill

Page 1

Performance Levels	Reading	Language	Mathematics	Science	Social Studies
5 Advanced					
4 Proficient	✓				
3 Nearing Proficiency	✓	✓	✓	✓	✓
2 Progressing (Partially Proficient)	✓	✓	✓	✓	✓
1 Step 1 (Partially Proficient)	✓	✓	✓	✓	✓

Observations

Performance level scores provide a measure of what students *can do* in terms of the content and skills assessed by *TerraNova*, and typically found in curricula for Grades 3, 4, and 5. It is desirable to work towards achieving a Level 4 (Proficient) or Level 5 (Advanced) by the end of Grade 5.

The number of check marks indicates the performance level this student reached in each content area. For example, this student reached Level 3 in Reading and Social Studies.

The performance level indicates this student can perform the majority of what is described for that level and even more of what is described for the levels below. The student may also be capable of performing some of the things described in the next higher level, but not enough to have reached that level of performance.

For example, this student can perform the majority of what is described for Level 3 in Reading and even more of what is described for Level 2 and Level 1 in Reading. This student may also be capable of performing some of what is described for Level 4 in Reading.

For each content area look at the skills and knowledge described in the next higher level. These are the competencies this student needs to demonstrate to show academic growth.

Copyright © 1997 CTB/McGraw-Hill. All rights reserved.

Figure 5 (SOURCE: CTB/McGraw-Hill, copyright © 1997. All rights reserved. Reproduced with permission.)

APPENDIX C

Performance Levels (Grades 3, 4, 5)	Reading	Language	Mathematics	Science	Social Studies
5 Advanced	Students use analogies to generalize. They identify/paraphrase of concepts or ideas in texts. They can indicate thought processes that led them to a previous answer. In written responses, they demonstrate understanding of an implied theme, assess intent of passage information, and provide justification as well as support for their answers.	Students understand logical development in paragraph structure. They identify essential information from notes. They recognize the effect of prepositional phrases on subject-verb agreement. They find and correct at least 4 out of 6 errors when editing simple narratives. They correct run-on and incomplete sentences in more complex texts. They can eliminate all errors when editing their own work.	Students locate decimals on a number line; compute with decimals and fractions; read scale drawings; find areas; identify geometric transformations; construct and label bar graphs find simple probabilities; find averages; use patterns in data to solve problems; use multiple strategies and concepts to solve unfamiliar problems; express mathematical ideas and explain the problem-solving process.	Students understand a broad range of grade-level scientific concepts, such as the structure of Earth and instinctive behavior. They know terminology, such as decomposers, fossil fuel, eclipse, and buoyancy. Knowledge of more complex environmental issues includes, for example, the positive consequences of a forest fire. Students can process and interpret more detailed tables and graphs. They can suggest improvements to experimental design, such as running more trials.	Students consistently demonstrate skills such as synthesizing information from two sources (e.g., a document and a map). They show understanding of the democratic process and global environmental issues, and know the location of continents and major countries. They analyze and summarize information from multiple sources in early American history. They thoroughly explain both sides of an issue and give complete and detailed written answers to questions.
4 Proficient	Students interpret figures of speech. They recognize paraphrase of text information and retrieve information to complete forms. In more complex texts, they identify themes, main ideas, or author purpose/point of view. They analyze and apply information in graphic and text form, make reasonable generalizations, and draw conclusions. In written responses, they can identify key elements from text.	Students select the best supporting sentences for a topic sentence. They use compound predicates to combine sentences. They identify simple subjects and predicates, recognize correct usage when confronted with two types of errors, and find and correct at least 3 out of 6 errors when editing simple narratives. They can edit their own work with only minor errors.	Students compare, order, and round whole numbers; know place value to thousands; identify fractions; use computation and estimation strategies; relate multiplication to addition; measure to nearest half-inch and centimeter; measure and find perimeters; estimate measures; find elapsed times; combine and subdivide shapes; identify parallel lines; interpret tables and graphs; solve two-step problems.	Students have a range of specific science knowledge, including details about animal adaptations and classification, states of matter, and the geology of Earth. They recognize scientific words such as habitat, gravity, and mass. They understand the usefulness of computers. They understand reasons for conserving natural resources. Understanding of experimentation includes analyzing purpose, interpreting data, and selecting tools to gather data.	Students demonstrate skills such as making inferences, using historical documents and global maps to determine the economic strengths of a region. They understand the function of currency in various cultures and supply and demand. They summarize information from multiple sources, recognize relationships, determine relevance of information, and show global awareness. They propose solutions to real-world problems and support ideas with appropriate details.
3 Nearing Proficiency	Students use context clues and structural analysis to determine word meaning. They recognize homonyms and antonyms in grade-level text. They identify important details, sequence, cause and effect, and lessons embedded in the text. They interpret characters' feelings and apply information to new situations. In written responses, they can express an opinion and support it.	Students identify irrelevant sentences in paragraphs and select the best place to insert new information. They recognize faulty sentence construction. They can combine simple sentences with conjunctions and use simple subordination of phrases/clauses. They identify reference sources. They recognize correct conventions for dates, closings, and place names in informal correspondence.	Students identify even and odd numbers, subtract whole numbers with regrouping; multiply and divide by one-digit numbers; identify simple fractions; measure with ruler to nearest inch; tell time to nearest fifteen minutes; recognize and classify common shapes; recognize symmetry; subdivide shapes; complete bar graphs; extend numerical patterns; apply simple logical reasoning.	Students are familiar with the life cycles of plants and animals. They can identify an example of a cold-blooded animal. They infer what once existed from fossil evidence. They recognize the term habitat. They understand the water cycle. They know science and society issues such as recycling and sources of pollution. They can sequence technological advances. They extrapolate data, devise a simple classification scheme, and determine the purpose of a simple experiment.	Students demonstrate simple information-processing skills in organizing information. They use time lines, product and global maps, and cardinal directions. They understand simple cause-and-effect relationships and historical documents. They sequence events, associate holidays with events, and classify natural resources. They compare life in different times and understand some economic concepts related to products, jobs, and the environment. They give some detail in written responses.
2 Progressing	Students identify synonyms for grade-level words, and use context clues to define common words. They make simple inferences and predictions based on text. They identify characters' feelings. They can transfer information from text to graphic form, or from graphic form to text. In written responses, they can provide limited support for their answers.	Students identify the use of correct verb tenses and supply verbs to complete sentences. They complete paragraphs by selecting an appropriate topic sentence. They select correct adjective forms.	Students know ordinal numbers; solve coin combination problems; count by tens; add whole numbers with regrouping; have basic estimation skills; understand addition property of zero; write and identify number sentences describing simple situations; read calendars; identify appropriate measurement tools; recognize congruent figures; use simple coordinate grids; read common tables and graphs.	Students recognize that plants decompose and become part of soil. They can classify a plant as a vegetable. They recognize that camouflage relates to survival. They recognize terms such as hibernate. They have an understanding of human impact on the environment and are familiar with causes of pollution. They find the correct bar graph to represent given data and transfer data appropriate for middle elementary grades to a bar graph.	Students demonstrate simple information-processing skills such as using basic maps and keys. They recognize simple geographical terms, types of jobs, modes of transportation, and natural resources. They connect a human need with an appropriate community service. They identify some early famous presidents and know the capital of the United States. Their written answers are partially complete.
1 Step 1 (Partially Proficient)	Students select pictured representations of ideas and identify stated details contained in simple texts. In written responses, they can select and transfer information from charts.	Students supply subjects to complete sentences. They identify the correct use of pronouns. They edit for the correct use of end marks and initial capital letters, and identify the correct convention for greetings in letters.	Students read and recognize numbers to 1000; identify real-world use of tens; add and subtract two-digit numbers without regrouping; identify addition situations; recognize and complete simple geometric and numerical patterns.	Students recognize basic adaptations for living in the water, identify an animal that is hatched from an egg, and associate an organism with its correct environment. They identify an object as metal. They have some understanding of conditions on the moon. They supply one way a computer can be useful. They associate an instrument like a telescope with a field of study.	Students are developing fundamental social studies skills such as locating and classifying basic information. They locate information in pictures and read and complete simple bar graphs related to social studies concepts and contexts. They can connect some city buildings with their functions and recognize certain historical objects.

IMPORTANT: Each performance level, depicted on the other side, indicates the student can perform the majority of what is described for that level and even more of what is described for the levels below. The student may also be capable of performing some of the things described in the next higher level, but not enough to have reached that level.

Figure 6 (SOURCE: CTB/McGraw-Hill, copyright © 1997. All rights reserved. Reproduced with permission.)

confidence interval. In these reports, we usually report either a 90 percent or 95 percent confidence interval. Interpret a confidence interval this way: Suppose we report a 90 percent confidence interval of 25 to 37. This means we estimate that, if the child took the test multiple times, we would expect that child's score to be in the 25 to 37 range 90 percent of the time.

Now look under the section titled Norm-Referenced Scores on the first page of the Individual Profile Report (Figure 3). The farthest column on the right provides the NP Range, which is the National Percentile scores represented by the score bands in the chart.

Next notice the column labeled Grade Equivalent. Theoretically, grade level equivalents equate a student's score in a skill area with the average grade placement of children who made the same score. Many psychologists and test developers would prefer that we stopped reporting grade equivalents, because they can be grossly misleading. For example, the average reading grade level of high school seniors as reported by one of the more popular tests is the eighth grade level. Does that mean that the nation's high school seniors cannot read? No. The way the test publisher calculated grade equivalents was to determine the average test scores for students in grades 4 to 6 and then simply extend the resulting prediction formula to grades 7 to 12. The result is that parents of average high school seniors who take the test in question would mistakenly believe that their seniors are reading four grade levels behind! Stick to the percentile in interpreting your child's scores.

Now look at the columns labeled Scale Score and National Stanine. These are two of a group of scores we also call *standard scores*. In reports for other tests, you may see other standard scores reported, such as Normal Curve Equivalents (NCEs), Z-Scores, and T-Scores. The IQ that we report on intelligence tests, for example, is a standard score. Standard scores are simply a way of expressing a student's scores in terms of the statistical properties of the scores from the norm group against which we are comparing the child. Although most psychologists prefer to speak in terms of standard scores among themselves, parents are advised to stick to percentiles in interpreting your child's performance.

Now look at the section of the report labeled Performance on Objectives. In this section, the test publisher reports how your child did on the various skills that make up each skills area. Note that the scores on each objective are expressed as a percentile band, and you are again told whether your child's score constitutes mastery, non-mastery, or partial mastery. Note that these scores are made up of tallies of sometimes small numbers of test items taken from sections such as Reading or Math. Because they are calculated from a much smaller number of scores than the main scales are (for example, Sentence Comprehension is made up of fewer items than overall Reading), their scores are less reliable than those of the main scales.

Now look at the second page of the Individual Profile Report (Figure 4). Here the test publisher provides a narrative summary of how the child did on the test. These summaries are computer-generated according to rules provided by the publisher. Note that the results descriptions are more general than those on the previous three report pages. But they allow the teacher to form a general picture of which students are performing at what general skill levels.

Finally, your child's guidance counselor may receive a summary report such as the TerraNova Student Performance Level Report. (See Figures 5 and 6.) In this report, the publisher explains to school personnel what skills the test assessed and generally how proficiently the child tested under each skill.

APPENDIX D

Which States Require Which Tests

Tables 1 through 3 summarize standardized testing practices in the 50 states and the District of Columbia. This information is constantly changing; the information presented here was accurate as of the date of printing of this book. Many states have changed their testing practices in response to revised accountability legislation, while others have changed the tests they use.

Table 1 State Web Sites: Education and Testing

STATE	GENERAL WEB SITE	STATE TESTING WEB SITE
Alabama	http://www.alsde.edu/	http://www.fairtest.org/states/al.htm
Alaska	www.educ.state.ak.us/	http://www.educ.state.ak.us/
Arizona	http://www.ade.state.az.us/	http://www.ade.state.az.us/standards/
Arkansas	http://arkedu.k12.ar.us/	http://www.fairtest.org/states/ar.htm
California	http://goldmine.cde.ca.gov/	http://star.cde.ca.gov/
Colorado	http://www.cde.state.co.us/index_home.htm	http://www.cde.state.co.us/index_assess.htm
Connecticut	http://www.state.ct.us/sde/	http://www.state.ct.us/sde/cmt/index.htm
Delaware	http://www.doe.state.de.us/	http://www.doe.state.de.us/aab/index.htm
District of Columbia	http://www.k12.dc.us/dcps/home.html	http://www.k12.dc.us/dcps/data/data_frame2.html
Florida	http://www.firn.edu/doe/	http://www.firn.edu/doe/sas/sasshome.htm
Georgia	http://www.doe.k12.ga.us/	http://www.doe.k12.ga.us/sla/ret/recotest.html
Hawaii	http://kalama.doe.hawaii.edu/upena/	http://www.fairtest.org/states/hi.htm
Idaho	http://www.sde.state.id.us/Dept/	http://www.sde.state.id.us/instruct/schoolaccount/statetesting.htm
Illinois	http://www.isbe.state.il.us/	http://www.isbe.state.il.us/isat/
Indiana	http://doe.state.in.us/	http://doe.state.in.us/assessment/welcome.html
Iowa	http://www.state.ia.us/educate/index.html	(Tests Chosen Locally)
Kansas	http://www.ksbe.state.ks.us/	http://www.ksbe.state.ks.us/assessment/
Kentucky	htp://www.kde.state.ky.us/	http://www.kde.state.ky.us/oaa/
Louisiana	http://www.doe.state.la.us/DOE/asps/home.asp	http://www.doe.state.la.us/DOE/asps/home.asp?I=HISTAKES
Maine	http://janus.state.me.us/education/homepage.htm	http://janus.state.me.us/education/mea/meacompass.htm
Maryland	http://www.msde.state.md.us/	http://msp.msde.state.md.us/
Massachusetts	http://www.doe.mass.edu/	http://www.doe.mass.edu/mcas/
Michigan	http://www.mde.state.mi.us/	http://www.MeritAward.state.mi.us/merit/meap/index.htm

APPENDIX D

STATE	GENERAL WEB SITE	STATE TESTING WEB SITE
Minnesota	http://www.educ.state.mn.us/	http://fairtest.org/states/mn.htm
Mississippi	http://mdek12.state.ms.us/	http://fairtest.org/states/ms.htm
Missouri	http://services.dese.state.mo.us/	http://fairtest.org/states/mo.htm
Montana	http://www.metnet.state.mt.us/	http://fairtest.org/states/mt.htm
Nebraska	http://www.nde.state.ne.us/	http://www.edneb.org/IPS/AppAccrd/ApprAccrd.html
Nevada	http://www.nde.state.nv.us/	http://www.nsn.k12.nv.us/nvdoe/reports/TerraNova.doc
New Hampshire	http://www.state.nh.us/doe/	http://www.state.nh.us/doe/Assessment/assessme(NHEIAP).htm
New Jersey	http://www.state.nj.us/education/	http://www.state.nj.us/njded/stass/index.html
New Mexico	http://sde.state.nm.us/	http://sde.state.nm.us/press/august30a.html
New York	http://www.nysed.gov/	http://www.emsc.nysed.gov/ciai/assess.html
North Carolina	http://www.dpi.state.nc.us/	http://www.dpi.state.nc.us/accountability/reporting/index.html
North Dakota	http://www.dpi.state.nd.us/dpi/index.htm	http://www.dpi.state.nd.us/dpi/reports/assess/assess.htm
Ohio	http://www.ode.state.oh.us/	http://www.ode.state.oh.us/ca/
Oklahoma	http://sde.state.ok.us/	http://sde.state.ok.us/acrob/testpack.pdf
Oregon	http://www.ode.state.or.us//	http://www.ode.state.or.us//asmt/index.htm
Pennsylvania	http://www.pde.psu.edu/	http://www.fairtest.org/states/pa.htm
Rhode Island	http://www.ridoe.net/	http://www.ridoe.net/standards/default.htm
South Carolina	http://www.state.sc.us/sde/	http://www.state.sc.us/sde/reports/terranov.htm
South Dakota	http://www.state.sd.us/state/executive/deca/	http://www.state.sd.us/state/executive/deca/TA/McRelReport/McRelReports.htm
Tennessee	http://www.state.tn.us/education/	http://www.state.tn.us/education/tsintro.htm
Texas	http://www.tea.state.tx.us/	http://www.tea.state.tx.us/student.assessment/
Utah	http://www.usoe.k12.ut.us/	http://www.usoe.k12.ut.us/eval/usoeeval.htm
Vermont	http://www.state.vt.us/educ/	http://www.fairtest.org/states/vt.htm

STATE	GENERAL WEB SITE	STATE TESTING WEB SITE
Virginia	http://www.pen.k12.va.us/Anthology/VDOE/	http://www.pen.k12.va.us/VDOE/Assessment/home.shtml
Washington	http://www.k12.wa.us/	http://www.k12.wa.us/assessment/
West Virginia	http://wvde.state.wv.us/	http://wvde.state.wv.us/
Wisconsin	http://www.dpi.state.wi.us/	http://www.dpi.state.wi.us/dpi/dltcl/eis/achfacts.html
Wyoming	http://www.k12.wy.us/wdehome.html	http://www.asme.com/wycas/index.htm

APPENDIX D

Table 2 Norm-Referenced and Criterion-Referenced Tests Administered by State

STATE	NORM-REFERENCED TEST	CRITERION-REFERENCED TEST	EXIT EXAM
Alabama	Stanford Achievement Test		Alabama High School Graduation Exam
Alaska	California Achievement Test	Alaska Benchmark Examinations	
Arizona	Stanford Achievement Test	Arizona's Instrument to Measure Standards (AIMS)	
Arkansas	Stanford Achievement Test		
California	Stanford Achievement Test	Standardized Testing and Reporting Supplement	High School Exit Exam (HSEE)
Colorado	None	Colorado Student Assessment Program	
Connecticut		Connecticut Mastery Test	
Delaware	Stanford Achievement Test	Delaware Student Testing Program	
District of Columbia	Stanford Achievement Test		
Florida	(Locally Selected)	Florida Comprehensive Assessment Test (FCAT)	High School Competency Test (HSCT)
Georgia	Stanford Achievement Test	Georgia Kindergarten Assessment Program—Revised and Criterion-Referenced Competency Tests (CRCT)	Georgia High School Graduation Tests
Hawaii	Stanford Achievement Test	Credit by Examination	Hawaii State Test of Essential Competencies
Idaho	Iowa Tests of Basic Skills/ Tests of Achievement and Proficiency	Direct Writing/Mathematics Assessment, Idaho Reading Indicator	
Illinois		Illinois Standards Achievement Tests	Prairie State Achievement Examination
Indiana		Indiana Statewide Testing for Educational Progress	
Iowa	(None)		
Kansas		(State-Developed Tests)	
Kentucky	Comprehensive Test of Basic Skills	Kentucky Core Content Tests	
Louisiana	Iowa Tests of Basic Skills	Louisiana Educational Assessment Program	Graduate Exit Exam
Maine		Maine Educational Assessment	High School Assessment Test
Maryland		Maryland School Performance Assessment Program, Maryland Functional Testing Program	

STATE	NORM-REFERENCED TEST	CRITERION-REFERENCED TEST	EXIT EXAM
Massachusetts		Massachusetts Comprehensive Assessment System	
Michigan		Michigan Educational Assessment Program	High School Test
Minnesota		Basic Standards Test	Profile of Learning
Mississippi	Comprehensive Test of Basic Skills	Subject Area Testing Program	Functional Literacy Examination
Missouri		Missouri Mastery and Achievement Test	
Montana	Iowa Tests of Basic Skills		
Nebraska			
Nevada	TerraNova		Nevada High School Proficiency Examination
New Hampshire		NH Educational Improvement and Assessment Program	
New Jersey		Elementary School Proficiency Test/Early Warning Test	High School Proficiency Test
New Mexico	TerraNova		New Mexico High School Competency Exam
New York		Pupil Evaluation Program/ Preliminary Competency Tests	Regents Competency Tests
North Carolina	Iowa Tests of Basic Skills	NC End of Grade Test	
North Dakota	TerraNova	ND Reading, Writing, Speaking, Listening, Math Test	
Ohio		Ohio Proficiency Tests	Ohio Proficiency Tests
Oklahoma	Iowa Tests of Basic Skills	Oklahoma Criterion-Referenced Tests	
Oregon		Oregon Statewide Assessment	
Pennsylvania		Pennsylvania System of School Assessment	
Rhode Island	Metropolitan Achievement Test	New Standards English Language Arts Reference Exam, New Standards Mathematics Reference Exam, Rhode Island Writing Assessment, and Rhode Island Health Education Assessment	
South Carolina	TerraNova	Palmetto Achievement Challenge Tests	High School Exit Exam
South Dakota	Stanford Achievement Test		
Tennessee	Tennessee Comprehensive Assessment Program	Tennessee Comprehensive Assessment Program	

APPENDIX D

STATE	NORM-REFERENCED TEST	CRITERION-REFERENCED TEST	EXIT EXAM
Texas		Texas Assessment of Academic Skills, End-of-Course Examinations	Texas Assessment of Academic Skills
Utah	Stanford Achievement Test	Core Curriculum Testing	
Vermont		New Standards Reference Exams	
Virginia	Stanford Achievement Test	Virginia Standards of Learning	Virginia Standards of Learning
Washington	Iowa Tests of Basic Skills	Washington Assessment of Student Learning	Washington Assessment of Student Learning
West Virginia	Stanford Achievement Test		
Wisconsin	TerraNova	Wisconsin Knowledge and Concepts Examinations	
Wyoming	TerraNova	Wyoming Comprehensive Assessment System	Wyoming Comprehensive Assessment System

Table 3 Standardized Test Schedules by State

STATE	KG	1	2	3	4	5	6	7	8	9	10	11	12	COMMENT
Alabama				X	X	X	X	X	X	X	X	X	X	
Alaska				X	X		X		X			X		
Arizona			X	X	X	X	X	X	X	X	X	X	X	
Arkansas					X	X		X	X		X	X	X	
California			X	X	X	X	X	X	X	X	X	X		
Colorado				X	X	X		X	X					
Connecticut					X		X		X					
Delaware				X	X	X			X		X	X		
District of Columbia		X	X	X	X	X	X	X	X	X	X	X		
Florida				X	X	X			X		X			There is no state-mandated norm-referenced testing. However, the state collects information furnished by local districts that elect to perform norm-referenced testing. The FCAT is administered to Grades 4, 8, and 10 to assess reading and Grades 5, 8, and 10 to assess math.
Georgia	X			X	X	X	X		X			X		
Hawaii				X			X		X		X			The Credit by Examination is voluntary and is given in Grade 8 in Algebra and Foreign Languages.
Idaho				X	X	X	X	X	X	X	X	X		
Illinois				X	X	X		X	X		X	X		Exit Exam failure will not disqualify students from graduation if all other requirements are met.
Indiana				X			X		X		X			
Iowa		*	*	*	*	*	*	*	*	*	*	*	*	*Iowa does not currently have a statewide testing program. Locally chosen assessments are administered to grades determined locally.
Kansas				X	X	X		X	X		X	X		

APPENDIX D

STATE	KG	1	2	3	4	5	6	7	8	9	10	11	12	COMMENT
Kentucky					X	X	X	X	X	X	X	X	X	
Louisiana				X	X	X	X	X	X	X	X	X	X	
Maine					X				X			X		
Maryland				X		X			X	X	X	X	X	
Massachusetts				X	X	X		X	X	X	X			
Michigan					X	X		X	X					
Minnesota				X		X			X	X	X	X	X	
Mississippi				X	X	X	X	X	X					Mississippi officials would not return phone calls or emails regarding this information.
Missouri			X	X	X	X	X	X	X	X	X			
Montana					X				X			X		The State Board of Education has decided to use a single norm-referenced test statewide beginning 2000–2001 school year.
Nebraska		**	**	**	**	**	**	**	**	**	**	**	**	**Decisions regarding testing are left to the individual school districts.
Nevada					X				X					Districts choose whether and how to test with norm-referenced tests.
New Hampshire				X			X				X			
New Jersey				X	X			X	X	X	X	X		
New Mexico					X		X		X					
New York				X	X	X	X	X	X	X			X	Assessment program is going through major revisions.
North Carolina	X			X	X	X	X		X	X			X	NRT Testing selects samples of students, not all.
North Dakota					X		X		X		X			
Ohio					X		X			X			X	
Oklahoma				X		X		X	X			X		
Oregon					X		X		X		X			

STATE	KG	1	2	3	4	5	6	7	8	9	10	11	12	COMMENT
Pennsylvania						X	X		X	X		X		
Rhode Island				X	X	X		X	X	X	X	X		
South Carolina				X	X	X	X	X	X	X	X	***	***	***Students who fail the High School Exit Exam have opportunities to take the exam again in grades 11 and 12.
South Dakota			X		X	X			X	X		X		
Tennessee			X	X	X	X	X	X	X					
Texas				X	X	X	X	X	X		X	X	X	
Utah		X	X	X	X	X	X	X	X	X	X	X	X	
Vermont					X	X	X		X	X	X	X		Rated by the Centers for Fair and Open Testing as a nearly model system for assessment.
Virginia				X	X	X	X		X	X		X		
Washington					X			X			X			
West Virginia				X	X	X	X	X	X	X	X	X		
Wisconsin					X				X		X			
Wyoming					X				X			X		

APPENDIX E

Testing Accommodations

The more testing procedures vary from one classroom or school to the next, the less we can compare the scores from one group to another. Consider a test in which the publisher recommends that three sections of the test be given in one 45-minute session per day on three consecutive days. School A follows those directions. To save time, School B gives all three sections of the test in one session lasting slightly more than two hours. We can't say that both schools followed the same testing procedures. Remember that the test publishers provide testing procedures so schools can administer the tests in as close a manner as possible to the way the tests were administered to the groups used to obtain test norms. When we compare students' scores to norms, we want to compare apples to apples, not apples to oranges.

Most schools justifiably resist making any changes in testing procedures. Informally, a teacher can make minor changes that don't alter the testing procedures, such as separating two students who talk with each other instead of paying attention to the test; letting Lisa, who is getting over an ear infection, sit closer to the front so she can hear better; or moving Jeffrey away from the window to prevent his looking out the window and daydreaming.

There are two groups of students who require more formal testing accommodations. One group of students is identified as having a disability under Section 504 of the Rehabilitation Act of 1973 (Public Law 93-112). These students face some challenge but, with reasonable and appropriate accommodation, can take advantage of the same educational opportunities as other students. That is, they have a condition that requires some accommodation for them.

Just as schools must remove physical barriers to accommodate students with disabilities, they must make appropriate accommodations to remove other types of barriers to students' access to education. Marie is profoundly deaf, even with strong hearing aids. She does well in school with the aid of an interpreter, who signs her teacher's instructions to her and tells her teacher what Marie says in reply. An appropriate accommodation for Marie would be to provide the interpreter to sign test instructions to her, or to allow her to watch a videotape with an interpreter signing test instructions. Such a reasonable accommodation would not deviate from standard testing procedures and, in fact, would ensure that Marie received the same instructions as the other students.

If your child is considered disabled and has what is generally called a Section 504 Plan or individual accommodation plan (IAP), then the appropriate way to ask for testing accommodations is to ask for them in a meeting to discuss school accommodations under the plan. If your child is not already covered by such a plan, he or she won't qualify for one merely because you request testing accommodations.

The other group of students who may receive formal testing accommodations are those identified as handicapped under the Individuals with Disabilities Education Act (IDEA)—students with mental retardation, learning disabilities, serious emotional disturbance, orthopedic handicap, hearing or visual problems, and other handicaps defined in the law. These students have been identified under procedures governed by federal and sometimes state law, and their education is governed by a document called the Individualized Educational Program (IEP). Unless you are under a court order specifically revoking your educational rights on behalf of your child, you are a full member of the IEP team even if you and your child's other parent are divorced and the other parent has custody. Until recently, IEP teams actually had the prerogative to exclude certain handicapped students from taking standardized group testing altogether. However, today states make it more difficult to exclude students from testing.

If your child is classified as handicapped and has an IEP, the appropriate place to ask for testing accommodations is in an IEP team meeting. In fact, federal regulations require IEP teams to address testing accommodations. You have the right to call a meeting at any time. In that meeting, you will have the opportunity to present your case for the accommodations you believe are necessary. Be prepared for the other team members to resist making extreme accommodations unless you can present a very strong case. If your child is identified as handicapped and you believe that he or she should be provided special testing accommodations, contact the person at your child's school who is responsible for convening IEP meetings and request a meeting to discuss testing accommodations.

Problems arise when a request is made for accommodations that cause major departures from standard testing procedures. For example, Lynn has an identified learning disability in mathematics calculation and attends resource classes for math. Her disability is so severe that her IEP calls for her to use a calculator when performing all math problems. She fully understands math concepts, but she simply can't perform the calculations without the aid of a calculator. Now it's time for Lynn to take the school-based standardized tests, and she asks to use a calculator. In this case, since her IEP already requires her to be provided with a calculator when performing math calculations, she may be allowed a calculator during school standardized tests. However, because using a calculator constitutes a major violation of standard testing procedures, her score on all sections in which she is allowed to use a calculator will be recorded as a failure, and her results in some states will be removed from among those of other students in her school in calculating school results.

How do we determine whether a student is allowed formal accommodations in standardized school testing and what these accommodations may be? First, if your child is not already identified as either handicapped or disabled, having the child classified in either group solely to receive testing accommodations will be considered a violation of the laws governing both classifications. Second, even if your child is already classified in either group, your state's department of public instruction will provide strict guidelines for the testing accommodations schools may make. Third, even if your child is classified in either group and you are proposing testing accommodations allowed under state testing guidelines, any accommodations must still be both *reasonable* and *appropriate*. To be reasonable and appropriate, testing accommodations must relate to your child's disability and must be similar to those already in place in his or her daily educational program. If your child is always tested individually in a separate room for all tests in all subjects, then a similar practice in taking school-based standardized tests may be appropriate. But if your child has a learning disability only in mathematics calculation, requesting that all test questions be read to him or her is inappropriate because that accommodation does not relate to his identified handicap.

Glossary

Accountability The idea that a school district is held responsible for the achievement of its students. The term may also be applied to holding students responsible for a certain level of achievement in order to be promoted or to graduate.

Achievement test An assessment that measures current knowledge in one or more of the areas taught in most schools, such as reading, math, and language arts.

Aptitude test An assessment designed to predict a student's potential for learning knowledge or skills.

Content validity The extent to which a test represents the content it is designed to cover.

Criterion-referenced test A test that rates how thoroughly a student has mastered a specific skill or area of knowledge. Typically, a criterion-referenced test is subjective, and relies on someone to observe and rate student work; it doesn't allow for easy comparisons of achievement among students. Performance assessments are criterion-referenced tests. The opposite of a criterion-referenced test is a norm-referenced test.

Frequency distribution A tabulation of individual scores (or groups of scores) that shows the number of persons who obtained each score.

Generalizability The idea that the score on a test reflects what a child knows about a subject, or how well he performs the skills the test is supposed to be assessing. Generalizability requires that enough test items are administered to truly assess a student's achievement.

Grade equivalent A score on a scale developed to indicate the school grade (usually measured in months of a year) that corresponds to an average chronological age, mental age, test score, or other characteristic. A grade equivalent of 6.4 is interpreted as a score that is average for a group in the fourth month of Grade 6.

High-stakes assessment A type of standardized test that has major consequences for a student or school (such as whether a child graduates from high school or gets admitted to college).

Mean Average score of a group of scores.

Median The middle score in a set of scores ranked from smallest to largest.

National percentile Percentile score derived from the performance of a group of individuals across the nation.

Normative sample A comparison group consisting of individuals who have taken a test under standard conditions.

Norm-referenced test A standardized test that can compare scores of students in one school with a reference group (usually other students in the same grade and age, called the "norm group"). Norm-referenced tests compare the achievement of one student or the students of a school, school district, or state with the norm score.

Norms A summary of the performance of a group of individuals on which a test was standardized.

Percentile An incorrect form of the word *centile*, which is the percent of a group of scores that falls below a given score. Although the correct term is *centile*, much of the testing literature has adopted the term *percentile*.

Performance standards A level of performance on a test set by education experts.

Quartiles Points that divide the frequency distribution of scores into equal fourths.

Regression to the mean The tendency of scores in a group of scores to vary in the direction of the mean. For example: If a child has an abnormally low score on a test, she is likely to make a higher score (that is, one closer to the mean) the next time she takes the test.

Reliability The consistency with which a test measures some trait or characteristic. A measure can be reliable without being valid, but it can't be valid without being reliable.

Standard deviation A statistical measure used to describe the extent to which scores vary in a group of scores. Approximately 68 percent of scores in a group are expected to be in a range from one standard deviation below the mean to one standard deviation above the mean.

Standardized test A test that contains well-defined questions of proven validity and that produces reliable scores. Such tests are commonly paper-and-pencil exams containing multiple-choice items, true or false questions, matching exercises, or short fill-in-the-blanks items. These tests may also include performance assessment items (such as a writing sample), but assessment items cannot be completed quickly or scored reliably.

Test anxiety Anxiety that occurs in test-taking situations. Test anxiety can seriously impair individuals' ability to obtain accurate scores on a test.

Validity The extent to which a test measures the trait or characteristic it is designed to measure. Also see *reliability*.

Answer Keys for Practice Skills

Chapter 2: Understanding Numbers and Patterns
1. B
2. A
3. D
4. A
5. D
6. C
7. B
8. D
9. D
10. C
11. C
12. A
13. B
14. A
15. B
16. A
17. B
18. C
19. D
20. A
21. C
22. A
23. A
24. B
25. C
26. D
27. B
28. B
29. C
30. B
31. C
32. C
33. C

Chapter 3: Addition
1. B
2. C
3. D
4. A
5. D
6. C
7. B
8. C
9. C
10. C
11. C
12. A
13. A
14. C
15. B
16. C
17. B
18. D
19. D
20. A
21. B
22. D
23. C
24. A
25. D

Chapter 4: Subtraction
1. B
2. C
3. A
4. B
5. B
6. B
7. C
8. B
9. C
10. C
11. B
12. C
13. B
14. C
15. D

Chapter 5: Time: Clocks and Calendars
1. A
2. B
3. B
4. B
5. B
6. C
7. A
8. C
9. A
10. B
11. A

Chapter 6: Money
1. A
2. C
3. A
4. B
5. B
6. A
7. C
8. D
9. C
10. A
11. B
12. C
13. A

Chapter 7: Geometry
1. B
2. C
3. C
4. B
5. D
6. A
7. C

8	C	8	C	9	B	4	B
9	A			10	A	5	C
		Chapter 9:		11	D	6	D
Chapter 8:		**Measurement**		12	D	7	D
Fractions		1	A			8	D
1	A	2	C			9	C
2	B	3	C	**Chapter 10:**		10	C
3	A	4	B	**Solving Word**		11	C
4	B	5	C	**Problems**		12	D
5	C	6	D	1	B	13	C
6	A	7	B	2	A	14	B
7	C	8	D	3	B	15	D

MATH, GRADE ONE

Sample Practice Test

You may be riding a roller coaster of feelings and opinions at this point. If your child has gone through the preceding chapters easily, then you're both probably excited to move on, to jump in with both feet, take the test, and that will be that. On the other hand, your child may have struggled a bit with some of the chapters. Some of the concepts may be difficult for him and will require a little more practice. Never fear!

All children acquire skills in all areas of learning when they are developmentally ready. We can't push them, but we can reinforce the skills they already know. In addition, we can play games and do activities to pave the way for their understanding of the skills that they will need to master later. With luck, that's what you've done with the preceding chapters.

The test that follows is designed to incorporate components of several different kinds of standardized tests. The test that your child takes in school probably won't look just like this one, but it should be sufficiently similar that he should be pretty comfortable with the format. The administration of tests varies as well. It is important that your child hear the rhythm and language used in standardized tests. If you wish, you may have your child read the directions that precede each test section to you first and explain what the item is asking him to do. Your child may try it on his own if you feel he understands it, or you may want to clarify the instructions.

Test Administration

If you like, you may complete the entire test in one day, but it is not recommended that your child attempt to finish it in one sitting. As test administrator, you'll find that you'll need to stretch, have a snack, or use the bathroom too! If you plan to do the test in one day, leave at least 15 minutes between sessions.

Before you start, prepare a quiet place, free of distractions. Have two or three sharpened pencils with erasers that don't smudge and a flat, clear work space. As your child proceeds from item to item, encourage him to ask if he doesn't understand something. In a real testing situation, questions are accepted, but the extent to which items can be explained is limited. Don't go overboard in making sure your child understands what to do. Your child will have to learn to trust his instincts somewhat.

The test shouldn't take all day. If your youngster seems to be dawdling along, enforce time limits and help him to understand that the real test will have time limits as well. Relax, and try to have fun!

MATH, GRADE ONE NAME AND ANSWER SHEET

To the Student:

These tests will give you a chance to put the tips you have learned to work. A few last reminders...

- Be sure you understand all the directions before you begin each test. You may ask the teacher questions about the directions if you do not understand them.

- Work as quickly as you can during each test.

- When you change an answer, be sure to erase your first mark completely.

- You can guess at an answer or skip difficult items and go back to them later.

- Use the tips you have learned whenever you can.

- It is OK to be a little nervous. You may even do better.

Now that you have completed the lessons in this book, you are on your way to scoring high!

Math, Grade One Name and Answer Sheet

Math Concepts

1 Ⓐ Ⓑ Ⓒ Ⓓ	13 Ⓐ Ⓑ Ⓒ Ⓓ	25 Ⓐ Ⓑ Ⓒ Ⓓ	37 Ⓐ Ⓑ Ⓒ Ⓓ	49 Ⓐ Ⓑ Ⓒ Ⓓ
2 Ⓐ Ⓑ Ⓒ Ⓓ	14 Ⓐ Ⓑ Ⓒ Ⓓ	26 Ⓐ Ⓑ Ⓒ Ⓓ	38 Ⓐ Ⓑ Ⓒ Ⓓ	50 Ⓐ Ⓑ Ⓒ Ⓓ
3 Ⓐ Ⓑ Ⓒ Ⓓ	15 Ⓐ Ⓑ Ⓒ Ⓓ	27 Ⓐ Ⓑ Ⓒ Ⓓ	39 Ⓐ Ⓑ Ⓒ Ⓓ	51 Ⓐ Ⓑ Ⓒ Ⓓ
4 Ⓐ Ⓑ Ⓒ Ⓓ	16 Ⓐ Ⓑ Ⓒ Ⓓ	28 Ⓐ Ⓑ Ⓒ Ⓓ	40 Ⓐ Ⓑ Ⓒ Ⓓ	52 Ⓐ Ⓑ Ⓒ Ⓓ
5 Ⓐ Ⓑ Ⓒ Ⓓ	17 Ⓐ Ⓑ Ⓒ Ⓓ	29 Ⓐ Ⓑ Ⓒ Ⓓ	41 Ⓐ Ⓑ Ⓒ Ⓓ	53 Ⓐ Ⓑ Ⓒ Ⓓ
6 Ⓐ Ⓑ Ⓒ Ⓓ	18 Ⓐ Ⓑ Ⓒ Ⓓ	30 Ⓐ Ⓑ Ⓒ Ⓓ	42 Ⓐ Ⓑ Ⓒ Ⓓ	54 Ⓐ Ⓑ Ⓒ Ⓓ
7 Ⓐ Ⓑ Ⓒ Ⓓ	19 Ⓐ Ⓑ Ⓒ Ⓓ	31 Ⓐ Ⓑ Ⓒ Ⓓ	43 Ⓐ Ⓑ Ⓒ Ⓓ	55 Ⓐ Ⓑ Ⓒ Ⓓ
8 Ⓐ Ⓑ Ⓒ Ⓓ	20 Ⓐ Ⓑ Ⓒ Ⓓ	32 Ⓐ Ⓑ Ⓒ Ⓓ	44 Ⓐ Ⓑ Ⓒ Ⓓ	56 Ⓐ Ⓑ Ⓒ Ⓓ
9 Ⓐ Ⓑ Ⓒ Ⓓ	21 Ⓐ Ⓑ Ⓒ Ⓓ	33 Ⓐ Ⓑ Ⓒ Ⓓ	45 Ⓐ Ⓑ Ⓒ Ⓓ	
10 Ⓐ Ⓑ Ⓒ Ⓓ	22 Ⓐ Ⓑ Ⓒ Ⓓ	34 Ⓐ Ⓑ Ⓒ Ⓓ	46 Ⓐ Ⓑ Ⓒ Ⓓ	
11 Ⓐ Ⓑ Ⓒ Ⓓ	23 Ⓐ Ⓑ Ⓒ Ⓓ	35 Ⓐ Ⓑ Ⓒ Ⓓ	47 Ⓐ Ⓑ Ⓒ Ⓓ	
12 Ⓐ Ⓑ Ⓒ Ⓓ	24 Ⓐ Ⓑ Ⓒ Ⓓ	36 Ⓐ Ⓑ Ⓒ Ⓓ	48 Ⓐ Ⓑ Ⓒ Ⓓ	

Math Computation

1 Ⓐ Ⓑ Ⓒ Ⓓ	5 Ⓐ Ⓑ Ⓒ Ⓓ	9 Ⓐ Ⓑ Ⓒ Ⓓ	13 Ⓐ Ⓑ Ⓒ Ⓓ	17 Ⓐ Ⓑ Ⓒ Ⓓ
2 Ⓐ Ⓑ Ⓒ Ⓓ	6 Ⓐ Ⓑ Ⓒ Ⓓ	10 Ⓐ Ⓑ Ⓒ Ⓓ	14 Ⓐ Ⓑ Ⓒ Ⓓ	18 Ⓐ Ⓑ Ⓒ Ⓓ
3 Ⓐ Ⓑ Ⓒ Ⓓ	7 Ⓐ Ⓑ Ⓒ Ⓓ	11 Ⓐ Ⓑ Ⓒ Ⓓ	15 Ⓐ Ⓑ Ⓒ Ⓓ	19 Ⓐ Ⓑ Ⓒ Ⓓ
4 Ⓐ Ⓑ Ⓒ Ⓓ	8 Ⓐ Ⓑ Ⓒ Ⓓ	12 Ⓐ Ⓑ Ⓒ Ⓓ	16 Ⓐ Ⓑ Ⓒ Ⓓ	20 Ⓐ Ⓑ Ⓒ Ⓓ

Math Applications

1 Ⓐ Ⓑ Ⓒ Ⓓ	5 Ⓐ Ⓑ Ⓒ Ⓓ	9 Ⓐ Ⓑ Ⓒ Ⓓ	13 Ⓐ Ⓑ Ⓒ Ⓓ	17 Ⓐ Ⓑ Ⓒ Ⓓ
2 Ⓐ Ⓑ Ⓒ Ⓓ	6 Ⓐ Ⓑ Ⓒ Ⓓ	10 Ⓐ Ⓑ Ⓒ Ⓓ	14 Ⓐ Ⓑ Ⓒ Ⓓ	18 Ⓐ Ⓑ Ⓒ Ⓓ
3 Ⓐ Ⓑ Ⓒ Ⓓ	7 Ⓐ Ⓑ Ⓒ Ⓓ	11 Ⓐ Ⓑ Ⓒ Ⓓ	15 Ⓐ Ⓑ Ⓒ Ⓓ	19 Ⓐ Ⓑ Ⓒ Ⓓ
4 Ⓐ Ⓑ Ⓒ Ⓓ	8 Ⓐ Ⓑ Ⓒ Ⓓ	12 Ⓐ Ⓑ Ⓒ Ⓓ	16 Ⓐ Ⓑ Ⓒ Ⓓ	20 Ⓐ Ⓑ Ⓒ Ⓓ

Cut along dashed line.

SAMPLE PRACTICE TEST

MATH CONCEPTS

Directions: Listen carefully to each question, and darken in the correct bubble on the separate answer sheet.

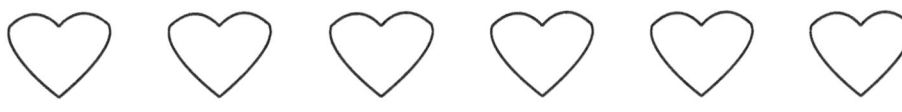

1 How many hearts are there in the picture above?

   A 3   **B** 4   **C** 6   **D** 7

2 Look at the picture above. Choose the group of objects below that has more than this number of stars?

A   **B**

C    **D**

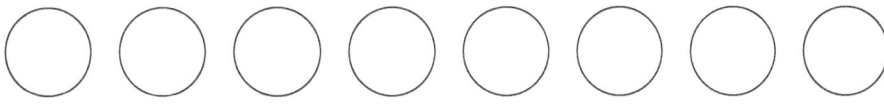

3 Look at the picture of circles above. Which picture has the same number of boxes as there are circles?

A    **B**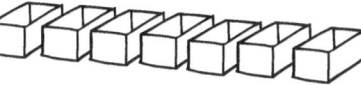

C 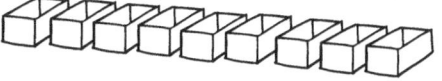   **D**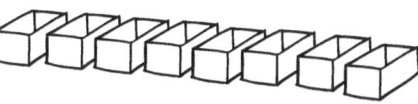

4 Look at the picture above. Choose the number word below that tells how many birds are in this set?

- **A** four
- **B** three
- **C** five
- **D** two

5 Look at the picture above. How many hats are needed to make the sets equal?

- **A** 3
- **B** 7
- **C** 4
- **D** 2

6 What number is missing? 15, 16, __, 18, 19

- **A** 16
- **B** 20
- **C** 17
- **D** 71

7 What number is between 46 and 48?

- **A** 48
- **B** 45
- **C** 49
- **D** 47

8 Which number is more than 17 and less than 25?

- **A** 17
- **B** 26
- **C** 16
- **D** 19

9 What number comes right before 61 when counting by ones?

- **A** 62
- **B** 60
- **C** 15
- **D** 16

10 Skip count by tens. Which number is missing? 60, 70, 80, __

- **A** 81
- **B** 50
- **C** 90
- **D** 85

Cut along dashed line.

11 Skip count by fives. What number is missing? 20, 25, __, 35

A 15

B 40

C 26

D 30

12 Skip count by twos. What number is missing? 2, __, 6, 8

A 3

B 10

C 9

D 4

13 Skip count by twos backward. What number is missing? 8, __, 4, 2

A 10

B 7

C 6

D 9

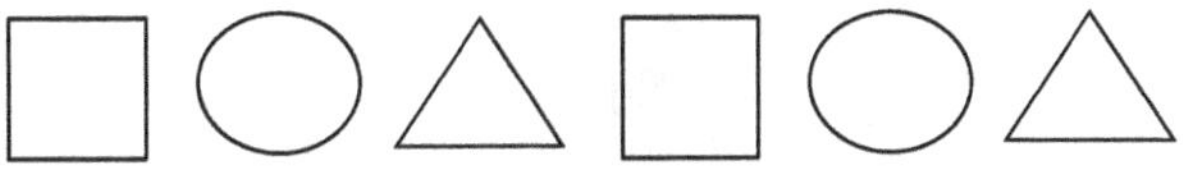

14 Continue the pattern.

A square

B circle

C triangle

D rectangle

15 What number has 3 tens and 7 ones?

A 10

B 30

C 73

D 37

16 How many tens are in the number 53?

A 8

B 3

C 5

D 2

17 What number is equal to 6 tens?

A 6

B 60

C 66

D 600

GO

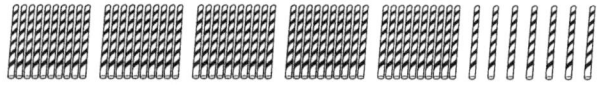

18 Look at the picture above. How many pencils are there in all?

A 3
B 30
C 33
D 300

19 These straws are in sets of tens and ones. How many are there in all?

A 57
B 12
C 75
D 55

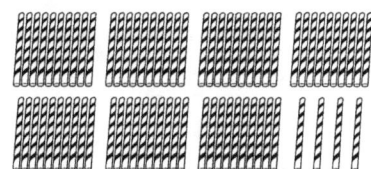

20 These straws are in sets of tens and ones. How many are there?

A 6 tens and 4 ones
B 4 tens and 7 ones
C 7 tens and 4 ones
D 11 tens and 11 ones

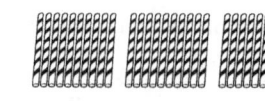 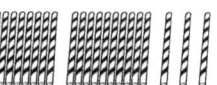

21 These straws are in sets of tens and ones. About how many are shown here?

A 10
B 50
C 20
D 40

22 Look at the picture above. Which car is black?

A first
B fourth
C third
D sixth

23 The number 8 is about how many?

A 2
B 10
C 15
D 5

24 Which one of the following numbers means the same as the number word for seventy-three?

- **A** 37
- **B** 67
- **C** 73
- **D** 7 + 3

25 Starting from the left, which animal is third?

- **A**
- **B**
- **C**
- **D**

26 What number sentence matches the picture above?

- **A** 5 − 3 = 2
- **B** 6 − 3 = 3
- **C** 8 − 5 = 3
- **D** 7 − 5 = 2

27 What number sentence matches the picture above?

- **A** 2 + 3 = 5
- **B** 3 + 3 = 6
- **C** 3 − 2 = 1
- **D** 4 + 2 = 6

MATH, GRADE ONE: GET READY!

28 How many more balloons than presents are there in the picture above?

    A   5 + 2 = 7

    B   5 − 3 = 2

    C   5 − 2 = 3

    D   5 + 3 = 8

29 What day of the week comes after Tuesday?

    A   Monday

    B   Saturday

    C   Friday

    D   Wednesday

30 How many days are in one week?

    A   5

    B   6

    C   7

    D   12

31 Look at the picture above. What time does the clock show?

    A   1:30

    B   12:30

    C   12:00

    D   1:00

32 Look at the clocks below. Choose the clock that shows 8:00.

A

B

C

D

GO

33 Look at the pictures below. Choose the coin worth ten cents.

A    B

C    D

34 Name the coin in the picture above.

A a quarter

B a dime

C a nickel

D a penny

35 Look at the coins above. How much are they worth all together?

A 30 cents

B 35 cents

C 25 cents

D 45 cents

36 Look at the coins above. How much are they worth all together?

A 16 cents

B 36 cents

C 31 cents

D 21 cents

JANUARY 2001						
Sunday	Monday	Tuesday	Wednesday	Thursday	Friday	Saturday
	1	2	3	4	5	6
7	8	9	10	11	12	13
14	15	16	17	18	19	20
21	22	23	24	25	26	27
28	29	30	31			

Directions: Use the calendar above to answer questions 37, 38, and 39.

37 How many days are in the month of January?

A 28

B 30

C 31

D 7

38 What day of the week is January 14?

A Sunday

B Tuesday

C Saturday

D Friday

39 How many Fridays are in the month?

A 4

B 31

C 7

D 3

40 How many sides does a triangle have?

A 2

B 4

C 3

D 5

41 Look at the shape above. Choose the name of this shape.

A triangle

B square

C rectangle

D circle

42 Look at the shapes below. Choose the cube.

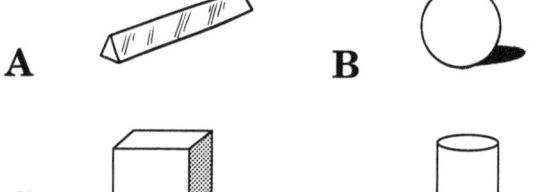

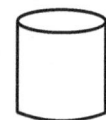

43 Look at the picture above. Which flat shape can be found on this cylinder?

A square

B rectangle

C circle

D triangle

44 Which object below has the same shape as this cylinder above?

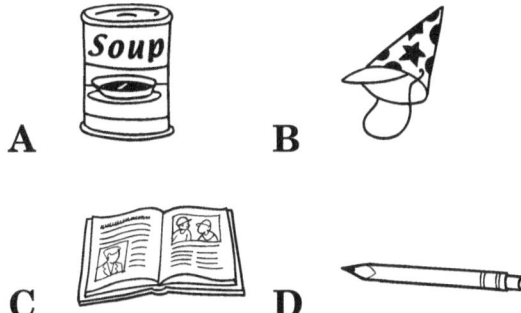

A   B

C   D

45 Which pictures shows two parts that match when folded on the dotted line?

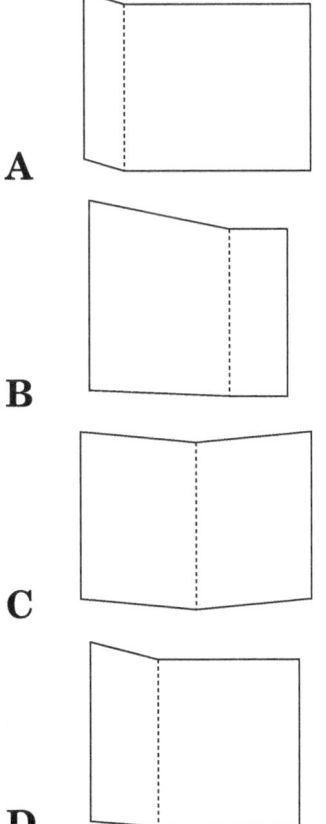

A

B

C

D

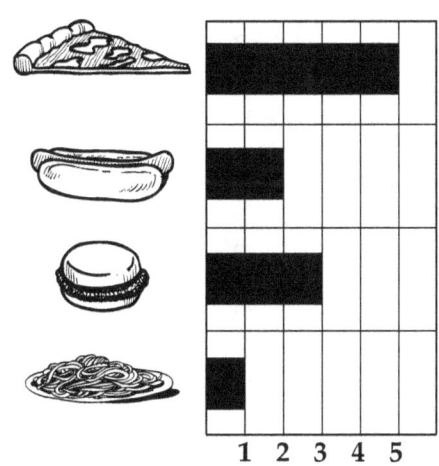

46 Look at the bar graph above. Which food is the most popular?

  A   hamburger

  B   hot dogs

  C   spaghetti

  D   pizza

47 In the bar graph in question 46, how many more children liked hamburgers than liked spaghetti?

  A   2

  B   3

  C   5

  D   1

48 Look at the shapes below. Which shows one-third?

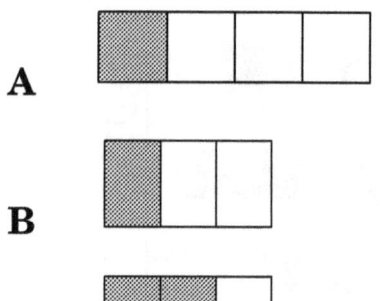

49 Which set below shows 1/4?

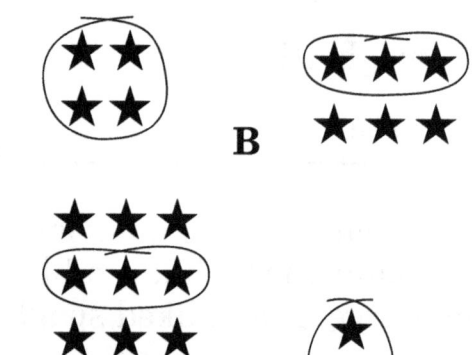

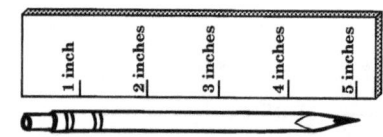

50 Look at the picture above. How long is the pencil?

    A 4 inches   **B** 5 inches

    C 3 inches   **D** 5 centimeters

51 Which picture below does not show fair shares?

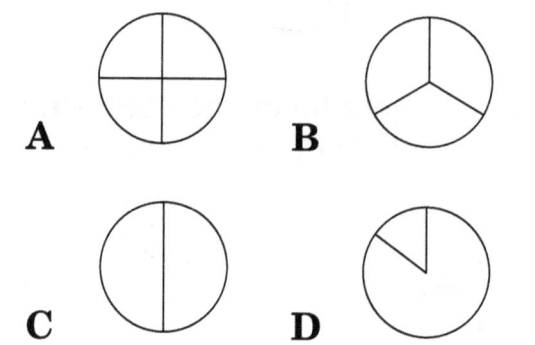

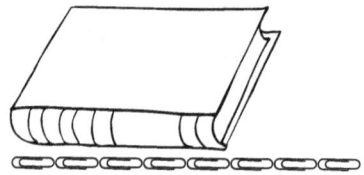

52 How long is the book in the picture above?

    A 5 paper clips long

    B 8 paper clips long

    C 6 paper clips long

    D 4 paper clips long

SAMPLE PRACTICE TEST

53 Which object weighs more than one pound?

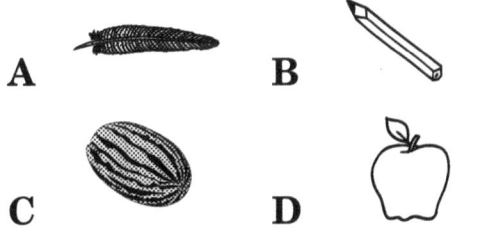

54 Which thermometer reading below would match the weather on a cold, snowy day?

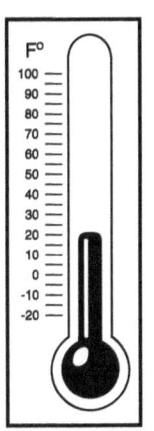
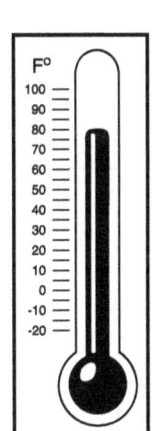

A   B

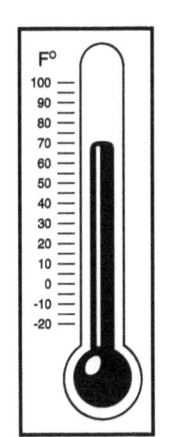
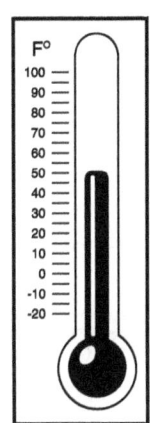

C   D

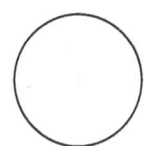

55 Which figure is the same size and shape as the one above?

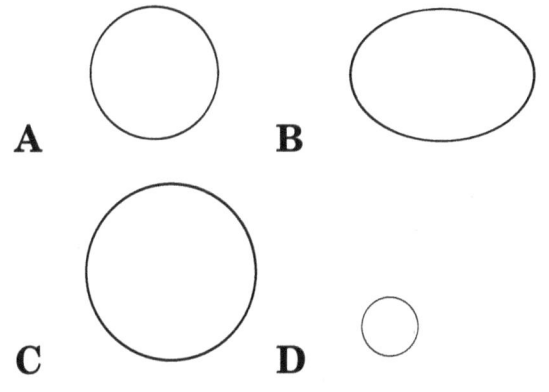

56 What measuring tool is used to measure laundry detergent?

A   a ruler

B   a scale

C   a thermometer

D   a cup

MATH COMPUTATION

1 3 + __ = 7

  A 2

  B 10

  C 4

  D 5

2 5 + 2 + 3 = __

  A 7

  B 8

  C 523

  D 10

3 12 + 4 = __

  A 6

  B 7

  C 16

  D 124

4 7 + 0 = __

  A 70

  B 7

  C 0

  D 8

5 12 − 5 = __

  A 13

  B 17

  C 7

  D 6

6 9 + 9 = __

  A 99

  B 0

  C 16

  D 18

7 8 − 4 = __

   A 12

   B 84

   C 4

   D 3

8 7 − 1 = __

   A 6

   B 71

   C 8

   D 7

9 67 − 12 = __

   A 79

   B 55

   C 75

   D 59

10 5 − 5 = __

   A 10

   B 0

   C 1

   D 55

11   6
    + 5

   A 1

   B 11

   C 9

   D 6

12   23
    + 16

   A 13

   B 39

   C 49

   D 38

13   4
      4
    + 3

   A 11

   B 8

   C 7

   D 10

14. 15
    − 7

    A 12
    B 6
    C 8
    D 4

15. 43
    + 52

    A 77
    B 95
    C 11
    D 52

16. 15
    − 6

    A 11
    B 21
    C 9
    D 12

17. 8 + 4 = __

    A 4   B 84
    C 12   D 11

18. 10 − 0 = __

    A 0
    B 10
    C 11
    D 100

19. 7 + 5 = __

    A 2
    B 12
    C 10
    D 13

20. 13 − 7 = __

    A 19
    B 14
    C 6
    D 5

MATH APPLICATIONS

1 Mario is having a birthday party at his house. His mother has tied balloons to the mailbox. There are 4 blue balloons and 3 pink balloons. How many balloons are there in all?

A 4 balloons

B 3 balloons

C 7 balloons

D 1 balloon

2 Zulma wants to buy some candy. She has 8 pennies, and she spends 2 pennies on candy. How many pennies does she have left?

A 8 pennies

B 10 pennies

C 5 pennies

D 6 pennies

3 There are 10 cats in the pet store and 3 dogs. How many more cats than dogs are there in the pet store?

A 13

B 10

C 6

D 7

4 Jin-Joo plays on her school baseball team. The team has 12 wooden bats. At the end of the season, Jin-Joo and her friends had broken 5 of them. How many bats does the team have left?

A 7 bats

B 13 bats

C 9 bats

D 17 bats

5 Ryan has a big card collection. He bought 24 baseball cards and 12 football cards. How many cards did he buy in all?

A 9 cards

B 26 cards

C 12 cards

D 36 cards

6 There are 45 girls and 33 boys in first grade. How many fewer boys than girls are there in first grade?

A 78

B 12

C 15

D 18

7 There are 17 bugs on a leaf in the Amazon rain forest. After a big gust of wind, 10 bugs fly away. How many bugs are left on the leaf?

A 27

B 7

C 9

D 5

---

8 Rosita just got her allowance. Her mother gave her one quarter. When she gets to the store, Rosita spends 12 cents for a small doll. How much money does she have left?

A 25 cents

B 12 cents

C 13 cents

D 8 cents

---

9 If a cookie cost 5 cents, how many can you buy with two dimes?

A 2

B 5

C 4

D 25

---

10 If your favorite TV show starts at 8:00 and is a half-hour long, what time does it end?

A 8:00

B 8:30

C 9:00

D 7:30

---

11 If Thuan is 3 years younger than Cheryl and Cheryl is 16, how old is Thuan?

A 13

B 19

C 14

D 12

---

12 Nancy got 6 pieces of candy from the piñata. She gave Lamont half of them. How many pieces did Nancy give to Lamont?

A 5

B 3

C 2

D 6

SAMPLE PRACTICE TEST

13 Bobby has 3 fish, Sabah has 1 fish, and Jennifer has 2 fish. How many fish do they have in all?

A 6

B 31

C 4

D 7

14 Carlitos and his father built three bookshelves for his room. Carlitos puts five books on each shelf. How many books does Carlitos have in all?

A 35

B 15

C 8

D 2

15 Denise has 4 baskets, and each basket has 2 stuffed teddy bears in it. How many teddy bears does she have in all?

A 6

B 2

C 8

D 10

16 Yong-Koo loves to collect cars. He has 21 toy cars. About how many toy cars does Yong-Koo have?

A 12

B 20

C 30

D 15

17 There are 7 candles on a cake. Timmy takes 2 candles. How many candles are left? Which number sentence matches the story?

A $7 + 5 = 12$

B $7 - 5 = 2$

C $7 - 2 = 5$

D $5 + 7 = 12$

18 Allison has 6 tennis balls and 4 tennis rackets. How many more tennis balls than tennis rackets does Allison have? Which number sentence matches the story?

A $6 + 4 = 10$

B $6 - 4 = 2$

C $10 - 6 = 4$

D $64 - 10 = 54$

SAMPLE PRACTICE TEST

19 If one book weighs 5 pounds, how much will 4 books weigh?

    A 54 pounds

    B 20 pounds

    C 9 pounds

    D 1 pound

20 If Eddie has 10 cents and he buys 2 lollipops that cost 3 cents each, how much money does he have left?

    A 6 cents

    B 10 cents

    C 4 cents

    D 2 cents

STOP

MATH, GRADE ONE

Answer Key for Sample Practice Test

Math Concepts

1	C
2	D
3	D
4	B
5	A
6	C
7	D
8	D
9	B
10	C
11	D
12	D
13	C
14	A
15	D
16	C
17	B
18	B
19	A
20	C
21	D
22	B
23	B
24	C
25	C
26	C
27	A
28	C
29	D
30	C
31	B
32	B
33	B
34	C
35	D
36	C
37	C
38	A
39	A
40	C
41	C
42	C
43	C
44	A
45	C
46	D
47	A
48	B
49	C
50	B
51	D
52	A
53	C
54	A
55	A
56	D

Math Computation

1	C
2	D
3	C
4	B
5	C
6	D
7	C
8	A
9	B
10	B
11	B
12	B
13	A
14	C
15	C
16	C
17	C
18	B
19	B
20	C

Math Applications

1	C
2	D
3	D
4	A
5	D
6	B
7	B
8	C
9	C
10	B
11	A
12	B
13	A
14	B
15	C
16	B
17	C
18	B
19	B
20	C

WORKSHEET

WORKSHEET

WORKSHEET

WORKSHEET

WORKSHEET

WORKSHEET

www.ingramcontent.com/pod-product-compliance
Lightning Source LLC
Chambersburg PA
CBHW080548170426

43195CB00016B/2713